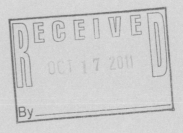

heart of the
artichoke
and other kitchen journeys

heart of the
artichoke
and other kitchen journeys

david tanis

PHOTOGRAPHS BY CHRISTOPHER HIRSHEIMER

ARTISAN
NEW YORK

Published by Artisan
A Division of Workman Publishing Company, Inc.
225 Varick Street
New York, NY 10014-4381
www.artisanbooks.com

Library of Congress Cataloging-in-Publication Data
Tanis, David.
Heart of the artichoke and other kitchen journeys / David Tanis.
    p. cm.
    ISBN 978-1-57965-407-8
1. Cookery, International. 2. Menus. 3. Entertaining. I. Title.
TX725.A1T334 2010
641.59—dc22
                                2010004538

Styling by Melissa Hamilton
Edited by Dorothy Kalins Ink, LLC
Design by Jan Derevjanik

Printed in Singapore
First printing, October 2010

1 3 5 7 9 10 8 6 4 2

Contents

A Little Disclaimer

Despite the title, this is not a book about artichokes. Or rather, it is and it isn't. There are some artichoke recipes within, though not terribly many.

What is an artichoke anyway? An unusual yet common vegetable that has been around for a very long time. We call it a vegetable, but actually it is the flower bud of a thistle. And I mean, really, who would ever think to eat a thistle? But there it is, and people have, for millennia.

The artichoke is ripe with metaphor and parable possibilities. Getting past the thorns to the sweet center, all of that. Not at all like reaching up and harvesting a sweet peach, eating an artichoke requires a bit of work.

For those willing to take the journey, the delicious heart is the prize at the end of the trail.

The Cuisine in My Head

I'm a restaurant chef who has always preferred to cook at home. Fortunately, the restaurant where I work, Chez Panisse, specializes in a cuisine that emulates the best of home cooking. In the downstairs dining room, a single menu is served nightly, changing with whims of the seasons and the weather and the availability of produce. So every day I get to design a menu quite similar to the kind of food I also cook at home— relatively simple dishes, somewhat traditional, fresh, clean, gutsy.

Still, I am happiest in my own home kitchen, and I like nothing better than gathering friends and family together for a meal.

A lot of people seem to be cooking and eating at home more these days, for different reasons. I view this as a good sign. I'm especially encouraged to see a new generation of cooks getting excited about home cooking, gardening, the seasonal approach, and the pleasures of the table. Food brings us together, nourishes us both literally and figuratively: time at the table is time well spent. Cooking for others is a generous and civilized act, even if it's just a simple pot of beans.

About This Book

In *Heart of the Artichoke,* there are three kinds of cooking—small, medium, and large.

In the first section, "Kitchen Rituals," I offer a quirky collection of small cooking moments. It's nice sometimes to cook only for oneself, or to make a small meal to share with a close companion. There are also times when a little kitchen project can be an enjoyable private endeavor. Some of the other rituals I describe are not so much about cooking as they are about savoring a food experience, whether it's eating tapas in Seville or oatmeal in Ohio.

Think of the seasonal menus that comprise the core of this book as medium-size cooking, meals for family and friends. These are menus for groups of 4 to 6. Most of them are easy to prepare, though some require some advance planning. Some are more appropriate for a weekend meal; all are satisfying and eminently doable.

Finally, "Simple Feasts for a Long Table," the chapter that ends the book, is about cooking large. These are menus for festive occasions. I find that for many people the leap from a small dinner party to a large one—for, say, 12 or 20—is pretty terrifying, but it needn't be. It may be a big table, but it doesn't have to be a big deal.

My style is to make menus that aren't terribly formal anyway, and in this book, I give some examples of utter informality. People don't always think in terms of three-course meals. This is fine! There's nothing wrong with having the table laden with food and just sitting down. All meals do not need to be served in courses. Sometimes a plate of potato salad and a cold beer *is* the meal, and sometimes a meal must be much more than that.

Time and the Cook

Also, you'll find that I have a lot to say about dishes that call for that elusive ingredient, time. I ask you to get your hands in the dough and to cultivate patience. Mesmerized by television shows hyping the thirty-minute meal and the blood sport of competitive cooking, we have somehow forgotten the pleasure of giving ourselves over to the true kitchen experience. This

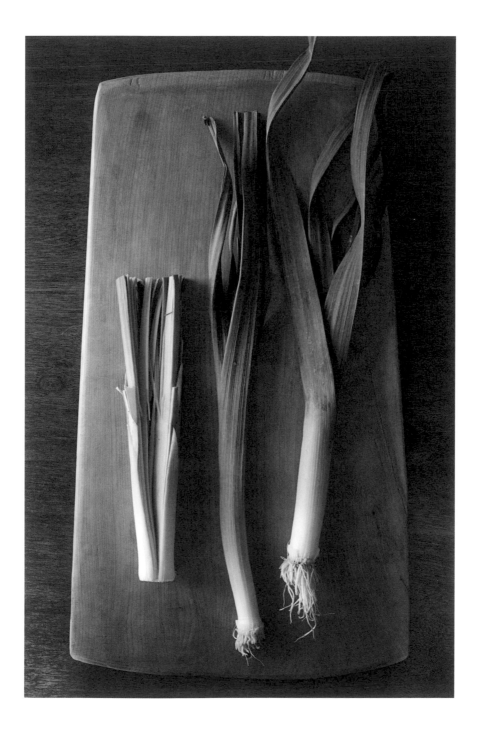

doesn't mean spending hours and hours in the kitchen. It's not more difficult cooking, but a different way of engaging with food. What matters is the joy that makes you part of a cooking continuum from beginning to end. It becomes a real journey. That journey is at the heart of *Artichoke.*

Regarding Kitchen Tools

People who've watched me cook, especially at home, say my hands are my two favorite tools. I do like to handle the food I cook, and I rely on just a few appliances and gadgets. I always say that a kitchen requires only fire, water, a worktable, and a sharp knife. A good vegetable peeler is handy, though, for things like potatoes. I like the French name for this tool—*l'économe*—which means it takes off the peel in an economical way, leaving as much of the carrot behind as possible.

A good mortar and pestle is a fine tool; it's old-fashioned, efficient, good for pounding garlic, spices, or herbs—or all three together, such as the seasonings to rub on a piece of pork (fennel seed, black peppercorns, garlic, sage, and rosemary, all pounded to a paste). I probably have a dozen tools for pounding, from the traditional Italian marble mortar to the Japanese *suribachi* and the deep ceramic mortars used in Thailand.

I know that many cooks rely on a food processor, but I am not much for electrical appliances. I make an exception for the blender, which is extremely useful for pureeing soups and salsas. Otherwise, give me a knife, a wooden spoon, and a cast-iron pan.

Something Sweet at the End of a Meal

I don't ever want a big, aggressive cake or pie or pastry after a good dinner. The old custom of taking sweets in the afternoon seems to me much more appropriate. And it makes sense—you get hungry and a little tired in the afternoon, and dinner is still a few hours away.

I like fruit after a meal. I love a bowl of tangerines, or plums, or grapes. If I'm serving a sweet at all, I'm inclined to have it be a little something along the lines of what used to be called sweetmeats—candied ginger or a single glacéed chestnut. I like the idea of a plate of small sweets, or dried fruits, or candied citrus peel, or Asian bean sweets, or small portions of those intensely sweet Middle Eastern desserts. A little bowl of ice cream or sherbet. Yogurt with honey or good jam is better for dessert than for breakfast. And I profess a great fondness for cookies, but not giant cookies, and not chocolate chip, and not oatmeal. Yet there are exceptions to all of these prejudices.

Good Ingredients

Pure and healthy ingredients are essential to good cooking. I encourage all cooks to do the best they can in this regard. The rewards are evident, both in flavor and in the effect on the environment. We owe our children and future generations a commitment to sustainable farming, and we affirm that commitment each time we prepare food with good ingredients.

Kitchen Rituals

Ordinary, private moments in the kitchen should be celebrated and savored. The smell of freshly brewed coffee and toasting bread is always heady. Peeling carrots and onions for a simple stew can be meditative. Boiling pasta while chopping garlic hits a primordial nerve. Washing lettuces in cool water is refreshing and relaxing. Are you cooking a fine humble meal for yourself? An omelette to share with a friend? Mixing up a batch of sausage? Making a small pot of jam?

Every cook has his rituals. Here are some of mine.

1.

Me and Aunt Jemima

Once, as it happened, I was house-sitting for friends and there was nothing in the house to eat. They did leave me a bottle of wine and a bottle of milk, but the refrigerator was bare. Just the milk and a couple of onions. I had jalapeños, because I always travel with them (see Ritual 6). Rooting through the cupboards was a disappointing journey: little bags of rancid walnuts, half-empty jars of store-bought jam, lots of instant ramen; none of that appealed.

And then I saw her: that familiar picture of Aunt Jemima smiling from a box of pancake mix. Jalapeño pancakes would be my simple supper! I sliced the jalapeños and the onions, mixed them with salt, cumin, and oil, and then added them to the thick batter. They were shockingly good, reminding me a bit of stuffed Indian naan. Now—sorry, Aunt Jemima—I make them from scratch. They are also excellent with fried eggs for breakfast or to accompany smoked salmon with a dab of sour cream.

JALAPEÑO PANCAKES: 1 cup all-purpose flour, 2 teaspoons baking powder, ½ teaspoon salt, 1 cup buttermilk, 1 egg, beaten, 1 tablespoon melted butter or olive oil; ½ cup thinly sliced onion or scallion, 1 or 2 jalapeño chiles, sliced thin, and ½ teaspoon toasted coarsely ground cumin.

Mix up the batter, and stir in the onion, jalapeños, and cumin. Heat up the griddle, and make your pancakes.

There used to be a time, before airplane security, when every fellow carried a pocketknife, useful for everything from whittling a toothpick to peeling an apple. The idea is to carefully conquer that apple, with a long spiral of skin as a trophy. It's mindful, it's a little bit silly, it's completely enjoyable.

Begin at the top of the apple, as close to the stem as you can, and start to peel, turning the fruit as you go. The goal is to remove as little flesh as possible, the knife hugging the skin. Ultimately, you could wind up with a two-foot-long ribbon of apple peel—or even longer, depending upon your patience and skill.

After you've thoroughly enjoyed the peeling of your apple, you cut it into wedges, remove the core, and share it. Or eat it by yourself with a piece of cheese. I know I'm not the only one who does this. It's the kind of thing a parent might show to a child. Maybe it's the fact that you can do it anywhere that appeals to me. And if it happens to be a new-crop apple in the fall, all the better. "My grandfather peeled oranges that way!" exclaimed Ignacio, my friend from Uruguay, when I peeled an apple for him recently.

You can peel a tangerine in a spiral too. It requires less skill and a thumbnail instead of a knife, and I've probably been doing this absentmindedly all my life. It works best with loose-skinned satsumas or clementines. And the spiral curl of peel can be rewound to reclaim its original shape. I would never think of peeling a tangerine any other way.

2.

Peeling an Apple

3.

Pasta for One

I was visiting my friend Kate in Berkeley one day and I was hungry. She served me some leftover pasta she'd made with pancetta and greens. I told her it was delicious. "Oh," she said, "it seemed a little dry, so I threw in a little lentil soup." That seemed to me an excellent idea. Sometimes your pasta just needs a little more of something, and you need to improvise. Kate made that decision and she was right.

I, too, have a favorite way of cooking pasta for one, though I didn't invent it. It's a bit like Spanish *fideos,* in which pasta is cooked like risotto and the broth is added in small increments. My version is rather soupy and littered with vegetables. I boil the pasta until it's half-done and cook the vegetables until they're half-done, then combine them and finish the cooking with a small amount of pasta water.

COOKING PASTA LIKE RISOTTO: Use short pasta like orecchiette or pennette. While the pasta is boiling, start the vegetables—they can be anything really, rough-chopped zucchini, artichokes, romano beans—in a skillet with a little olive oil, onion, garlic, pancetta (or not), perhaps a little tomato. When the vegetables and pasta are both half-cooked, add the pasta to the skillet, along with a ladle of pasta water. Keep the pan at a brisk simmer, stirring occasionally, and adding pasta water as necessary. Taste the resulting broth to make sure it is lively, bright, and well seasoned. Then, when the pasta is al dente and the vegetables are cooked to your liking, pour it all into a wide bowl. It can be quite brothy, or not very, and tastes best eaten with a big spoon The whole process takes about 15 minutes.

When I was growing up, there were oatmeal days (I preferred these), and there were Cream of Wheat days. The Cream of Wheat box had a man in a puffy chef's hat who seemed to me to be related to Uncle Ben. The oatmeal came in a cardboard cylinder with a picture of the Quaker Oats man on the front. These oats were quick-cooking: a little water and a pinch of salt, and only 10 minutes. Each bowl was presented with a pat of margarine in the center, then every family member added his own milk and sugar. I had strong feelings about the amount of milk.

I liked a discernible mound of oatmeal, always well exposed, with a shallow moat of milk around that island. Then I'd add a small spoonful of sugar directly over the margarine. I still remember the too-sweet taste of white sugar and milk.

A little bit of extra margarine would run down into the milk, so I'd get a little "buttery" milk with every bite. But the trick was this: starting with my spoon at 9 o'clock, I'd begin to eat the oatmeal with a little bit of the milk moat, always working to the edges of the bowl. And the way I did that was to eat from the moat in a counterclockwise direction while spinning the bowl with my left hand in a clockwise direction. I'd continue eating while rotating the bowl, occasionally adding a little more milk to the moat if necessary. At the end of the process, I had a prize: a sugary lump of margarine-laden oatmeal, saved until the very end.

Of course, this was a child's rite, and I rarely eat oatmeal these days. But damned if I don't find myself eating a bowl of polenta in the same circular fashion.

4.

Eating Oatmeal

5.

Beans on Toast

This is emphatically not that British idea where canned, sweetened baked beans are piled on toasted store-bought white bread for a student's frugal meal, or as part of a full English breakfast. I'm talking about something that's neither soup nor sandwich, but a bit of each—a slice of crispy bread topped with slow-cooked beans, warm and steamy on the plate. I never developed a taste for baked beans, perhaps because I didn't grow up with them. But I sure did develop a taste for slow-cooked Italian cannellini, or great northern or garbanzo beans, simmered with a little olive oil, rosemary, and garlic.

I don't want to sound like a snob, but beans in a can have no soul. There are a few places—like La Boqueria in Barcelona—where there's a woman who sells nothing but cooked beans, ready to take home and heat up. And in Italy there are vendors who have precooked beans—along with blanched greens, squeezed into balls, and trimmed artichokes—for home cooks pressed for time. In the States, not so much, although you can find cooked pinto beans in most Mexican markets.

If you're in dire straits, you can try for this goodness with a can of doctored beans. But it's so much better to make a small pot of cooked beans. You start with beans on toast on the first day, eaten warm from the pot. The next day it could be a bean salad, and on the third day, it's bean soup. In the summertime, you can use fresh shelling beans.

SIMMERING THE BEANS: Put a pound of dried cannellini beans, a small sprig of rosemary, a few garlic cloves, and a pinch of red pepper flakes in a pot. Cover with water and simmer slowly for 2 hours. Add a good pinch of salt after the first hour. When the beans are soft and creamy inside, toast a thick slice of good country bread. Lay the toast in a soup bowl, and spoon the beans over the toast with a little of the bean broth. Drizzle liberally with olive oil, and sprinkle with salt, pepper, and a few red pepper flakes.

Good food on the road is hard to find and what there is often needs a little help. I've learned the hard way the atrocities of airport fare, the horrors of the minibar. I always try to pack a food kit, with an assortment of condiments. It's a kind of traveling pantry to check in my bag, keep handy in the car, or save for a hotel picnic. This is in addition to a deliberately prepared little snack to take on the plane, or smoked salmon sandwiches and white wine in a hamper for a two-hour train ride. Think of it as food insurance—a way to reward yourself for suffering the endless indignities of travel.

MY TRAVELING PROVISIONS: A tube of harissa, the spicy Moroccan paste that's better than most commercial hot sauces; a jar of good mustard; a few fresh chiles; a couple of limes; a little packet of sea salt, and one of red pepper flakes; a pepper mill; a hunk of cheese; a paring knife; and a corkscrew. You get the idea.

6.

Harissa to Go

7.

Hooray for Ziploc Bags

I usually think of myself as a pretty traditional, backward-tending romantic type, but I do believe Ziploc bags are a genius invention and I wish I owned the patent. A catering friend clued me in to their indispensability—she stores things that usually take up space in bins and boxes in big Ziplocs with the air squeezed out. And ever since, I've used them for freezing a quart of chicken stock (it packs very flat), homemade jam, or, surprisingly, ripe summer tomatoes. After years of steamy canning parties, preserving tomatoes in a Ziploc bag has become a cool and welcome ritual. When you thaw your tomatoes, the skin will come off easily, and you'll have peeled tomatoes all year long, fresher tasting than from a can. And always ready for a quick tomato sauce, a soup, or a stew.

FREEZER CANNING: Start with sweet, ripe garden tomatoes that actually taste like something. Put whole tomatoes, skin and all, into a Ziploc freezer bag. Squash the tomatoes in the bag to release the air and make the bag flat.

I remember the first time I ate a fresh artichoke, in faraway California. I had certainly never even seen one when I was growing up in the Midwest. Even the ones in jars at the supermarket were foreign to us.

On the West Coast they were considered normal—everyday fare, but fun to eat nonetheless. Picking off the leaves and dipping them in some kind of sauce—mayonnaise, vinaigrette, or melted butter, depending on whose house—was an easy ritual to love.

Nowadays, my ritual is to eat them raw, a habit I picked up in the South of France . . . or was it Milan? There they have the lovely little *violets de Provence.* Similar to the so-called baby artichokes available in North America, these small artichokes have no hairy choke. You simply peel away a few outer leaves to reveal the tender pale interior. In a few quick motions, you can trim the stem end and thinly slice the artichoke. Two or three little artichokes are enough for lunch. Simply season the raw slices with salt and pepper, drizzle with good olive oil and a squeeze of lemon, and toss with a few parsley leaves or some arugula. Add Parmigiano shavings if you wish.

8.

Raw Artichokes for Lunch

9.

Ham Sandwich in a French Bar

A well-made sandwich is a superb thing, and not so easy to find in the world, despite the fact that so-called panini seem to be all too available everywhere. Why is it so difficult to get a good sandwich? So many are too complicated or slapped together, ill-considered.

If, for instance, you happen to be in Paris, you can still walk into nearly any bar and get a simple ham sandwich on a fresh baguette, and it will somehow be just right. Fresh bread, good butter, good ham. That's *it*. If you want mustard or cornichons, they'll be served on the side. This is where a premade, plastic-wrapped sandwich goes wrong. A flawless sandwich must be built to order, quickly but perfectly. Not piled with lettuce, tasteless tomatoes, or sprouts and whatever. Just streamlined. Simple. The same sort of simplicity you get in Italy with prosciutto on a roll, or in Spain with *jamón*. If you crave something more complex, head for a Vietnamese neighborhood for a *bánh mì,* a stellar sandwich with an Asian sensibility that adds strips of lightly pickled carrot and cucumber and hot green chile.

A SIMPLE SANDWICH: One really good baguette, some fresh sweet butter, the best cooked ham or *jambon de pays* you can find. Split the baguette, butter it generously, lay in the ham. *Et voilà!*

10.

Making a Little Jam

Apricot is the ne plus ultra, the cat's meow, of jam, and part of the thrill of making it is to take advantage of the brief apricot season. If you have 2 cups of apricots and 2 cups of sugar, in a short while you'll have the most unctuous jam. Don't be tempted to cut back on the sugar: no matter how good they taste eaten out of hand, even very ripe apricots will never be sweet enough for jam, and their flavor will not come through without ample sugar.

Although I don't consider myself a person with a real sweet tooth, when it comes to bread and butter and jam, that's a different story. This jam tastes best the week it's made. I am not making it for posterity, I am making it for breakfast. A jar goes in the fridge, and a couple of other jars go for gifts. No big production. But oh so satisfying.

There are four jams I like to make the most: apricot; fig; blackberry, especially wild; and Italian plum. The method is pretty much the same for all of them.

A SMALL BATCH OF APRICOT JAM: Halve the apricots but don't peel them. Remove the pits. Put the apricots and sugar in a heavy-bottomed pot. Stir the apricots together with the sugar first, to moisten the sugar. Then put the pot on the heat and add ½ cup water to help get the process going. When the sugar's dissolved, turn the heat to medium and bring the pot to a brisk simmer. It will smell really, really good and look even better. A lovely apricot-colored foam will rise to the surface. Skim off the foam and spread it on toast, or add a spoonful to a little bowl of yogurt.

Turn the heat down a bit, but keep the jam simmering, stirring frequently. After 30 minutes, it should start to look right (judging by eye is the key to making this jam) and will coat a spoon.

Take the pot off the stove and let the jam cool overnight at room temperature. The next day, if it looks a little thin, put the jam back on the stove and let it cook for another 15 minutes or so. Too thick, add a bit of water and simmer it until the consistency's right. Ladle into jars and refrigerate.

11.

Mexican Breakfast

The Mexican dish chilaquiles is a quick, satisfying breakfast made from leftover tortillas. Every cook makes chilaquiles differently. Sometimes it's lightly fried strips of day-old tortilla, mixed with a spicy tomato salsa and served as an accompaniment to fried eggs. Other versions are long simmered and quite saucy, and some add meat, usually chicken. My go-to variation is more like a cross between a stir-fry and scrambled eggs.

BREAKFAST FOR ONE: Cut 4 day-old corn tortillas into strips. Heat a cast-iron skillet, add a little vegetable oil or lard, add the tortilla strips and a little salt, and stir to coat them. The tortilla strips will wilt, then crisp, which is what you want. Throw in a big handful of chopped cilantro, scallions, and chopped jalapeños and stir them around. Add a spoonful of red or green salsa if you like. Now add 2 beaten eggs seasoned with salt and pepper. Mix and stir the eggs with the tortillas until the eggs are set. Finish the chilaquiles with a little crumbled queso fresco.

I've been hooked on herring since childhood. My mother always served herring in sour cream for company, as an appetizer on rye bread. Years later, I found that the best thing to eat in Amsterdam was a herring fillet with onions, on a bun, sold from kiosks all over town—better than a hot dog.

One of my favorite dishes in Paris is the traditional brasserie standby of good boiled potatoes drenched in oil (*pommes à l'huile*) with sweet, meaty, cold marinated herring (*hareng*). It makes a fine treat year-round and it's easy to make at home for one or two.

The hard part is locating the herring. The herring in jars at the supermarket won't do—too many added seasonings. Some old-fashioned delis carry mild matjes herring in brine, and that's what you want. Lacking that, you can still make this salad using kippers (cold smoked herring) or smoked trout.

HERRING AND POTATO SALAD: Slice a carrot thinly and boil it in salted water with a bay leaf, a thyme sprig, and a splash of vinegar. Drain and cool. Put the slices in a bowl and add a few thin slices of sweet onion, a little salt, and a drop of vinegar. Rinse 2 herring fillets, pat dry, and cut into wide chunks. Add the herring to the carrots, drizzle with olive oil and freshly ground black pepper, and mix gently. Chill.

Boil 1 pound of medium potatoes (you want a tasty firm-fleshed boiling potato such as Yellow Finn or Yukon Gold) in their jackets until tender. While they're still warm, peel and slice them thickly. Put the slices in a low serving dish in one layer, sprinkle lightly with red wine vinegar, salt, and pepper, and drizzle generously with good olive oil. Let them sit for a half hour. Then top the potatoes with the marinated herring mixture, chopped parsley, and scallions.

12.

Herring and Potatoes

13.

A Bowl of Tripe

There's the pleasure of making tripe, and then there's the private ritual it inevitably becomes because you can't get anyone to eat it with you. Which is sort of sad, because for me, a bowl of tripe has the same comforting value as chicken soup.

Take 2 or 3 pounds of tripe and a sharp knife. I love to see the tripe there on my cutting board, all white and frilly. As I slice it into thin ribbons (discarding gristle and fat), I think of the tripe dishes I have savored in the past: cold Chinese tripe dim sum with sesame oil; Spanish *callos* with chorizo; Roman-style tripe with tomato and Parmigiano; Florentine-style, boiled, on a bun; spicy Mexican *menudo,* the hangover cure. And, of course, the French *tripe à la mode de Caen.*

First boil the sliced tripe in a big pot of salted water for about 20 minutes. Then drain it as if you were draining pasta.

Dice a large onion, slice 6 cloves of garlic, and soften them in olive oil in a sturdy stew pot. Stir in the drained tripe, and season well with salt and pepper. Add a bay leaf, a clove, and a sprig of thyme, then add water to cover by 2 inches. Cover and simmer gently for at least an hour, until the tripe is extremely tender. Taste the broth and adjust the seasonings. Pour the tripe and all its liquid into a Pyrex dish and refrigerate overnight until it firms into a solid block. The next day, you'll have basic cooked tripe, which can be transformed into wonderful things.

To serve it Roman-style, heat up a portion of the boiled tripe, add half a cup of homemade tomato puree and a pinch of red pepper flakes, and simmer for 15 or 20 minutes. Make it as spicy as you like—I think it should be quite zippy and peppery. Pour the tripe into a soup bowl and sprinkle with freshly grated cheese— Parmigiano or pecorino romano.

14.

A Batch of Spanish Chorizo

Making chorizo always gives me true satisfaction. The simple combination of red pepper, garlic, and pork produces an authentic Spanish flavor that transports me immediately to the Iberian peninsula. But the process is wonderful, too. It smells so good, you know the end result will be great. I love looking at the sausages as they hang about my kitchen. While they hang and lose weight, the sausages wrinkle and dry, concentrating the flavor.

You can use the sausages for everything. Slice one into small rounds and warm it in a pan until it releases its delicious fat, beautiful color, and distinctly Spanish aroma. Break a few eggs into the pan and stir up some soft-scrambled eggs with chorizo. Or add wedges of boiled potatoes (or cubes of bread) to the sausage in the pan and brown them gently. Delicious! Use chorizo in place of ham or bacon in a bean soup; it goes with every kind of bean you can imagine, from lentils to garbanzos to giant white beans. I like to make a quick sauté of chorizo, sweet peppers, onions, and chicken livers flavored with a little sherry. And a little chorizo added to a dish of steamed clams is sensational too.

My recipe comes from a Gypsy named Anzonini who used to live in Berkeley. He gave it to Kenny, a flamenco guitar player, who gave it to me.

MAKING CHORIZO: To make the sausages, gather these ingredients: 6 large dried ancho or New Mexico chiles; 5 pounds boneless pork shoulder, not too lean; 1 head garlic, peeled and chopped; 1 tablespoon peppercorns, crushed; ¾ cup good-quality paprika; 1 tablespoon salt; 1 teaspoon curing salt (optional); and a length of hog casings.

Cut the chiles lengthwise in half and remove the seeds and stems. Cover with cold water in a saucepan and simmer for about 10 minutes, until the chiles are soft. Let cool in the broth, then grind them to a thick puree in a blender, using a little of the cooking water. Reserve the rest of the cooking water.

Grind three-quarters of the pork very coarsely, or hand-chop it. Grind the remaining quarter medium-fine. In a large mixing bowl, combine all the meat, the garlic, peppercorns, paprika, salt, and curing salt,

if using. Mix with your hands, making sure that the seasonings are well distributed. Add the chile puree and a cup of the cooled reserved cooking water and mix well. Cover the bowl, refrigerate, and let the flavors ripen overnight.

Rinse the casings well, then stuff them with the sausage mixture. You can use a meat grinder with a sausage horn (some standing mixers have sausage-making attachments), or order equipment from a sausage-making supply company. But it's not difficult to do it the old-fashioned way, using a large funnel, and stuffing the casings by hand.

Make the links about 12 inches long, twisting little spaces between the links to compress the meat and give you a place to hang them from. Hang at cool room temperature for about a week before using. (If you're not using the curing salt, hang them from a rack in the refrigerator.) Lay down newspaper below your hanging sausages; they'll drip for a couple of days.

A batch of chorizo will keep for a month or so in the fridge. Keep them loosely wrapped in parchment or wax paper. They'll continue to dry a bit, but that's fine.

Spring Menus

menu one

SPRING LAMB

Asparagus-Scrambled Eggs

Fork-Mashed Potatoes

Spring Lamb with Rosemary

Dandelion Greens Salad

Strawberries with Sugar and Cream

menu two

RECLAIMING ARUGULA

Fennel Soup with a Green Swirl

Pork Scaloppine with Lemon, Capers, and Chopped Arugula

Zucchini Pancakes

Italian Spice Cake

Tangerines

menu three

IN A SICILIAN KITCHEN

Sicilian Salad

Pasta "Timballo" with Fresh Ricotta

Fried Puffs with Honey (Sfince)

menu four

THE FLAVOR OF SMOKE

Scallion Broth

Tea-Smoked-Chicken Salad with Ginger Vinaigrette

Sesame Peanut Candy

menu five

FEELING VIETNAMESE

Vegetable Rice Paper Rolls

Pho (Vietnamese Beef Soup)

Black Sticky Rice Pudding with Coconut Cream

Spring Lamb

Asparagus-Scrambled Eggs
Fork-Mashed Potatoes
Spring Lamb with Rosemary
Dandelion Greens Salad
Strawberries with Sugar and Cream

Chefs nowadays want to dazzle. I suppose they always have. Not to denigrate modern cooking—I don't mean to squelch the creative urge—but one has to wonder sometimes about what restaurant food has become. Armed with all manner of machinery, it seems the modern chef now wants to do battle with an instant foam maker, a centrifugal food puree-er, a fast-freezing device, and a blowtorch. And a growing number of food professionals favor slow-cooking in plastic pouches. The simple hands-on approach to cooking has given way to the laboratory, futuristic flavored "air," and edible "art." To be sure, not all modern chefs have succumbed. But even so, traditional cooks are now seen as backward, and modern diners want excitement—two bites and they're bored.

Last spring I attended a symposium of chefs from all over Europe who had gathered to explore modern food; *la cuisine jeune,* they called it—young cooking. This was the Omnivore Food Festival, held at a seaside conference center in Deauville, France. The place was packed, each dish was applauded enthusiastically, and every chef was ovated, sometimes standingly. To a man (and they were all men), the chefs professed a love of simple food, of seasonal ingredients, of traditional cooking. And yet, you just have to hear what they cooked.

An Italian chef claimed his dish delivered a sense memory equal to his mama's *ravioli di zucca:* she sweetened a pumpkin filling for pasta with amaretti cookies, added salt with Parmigiano. His updated version involved making a puree of pumpkin and yucca root, seasoned with the Japanese citrus yuzu. This puree was troweled to a thickness of one-sixteenth of an inch and left to dry overnight. The next day, it was ripped into shards, fried lightly in olive oil, and showered with grated Parmigiano. But not just any Parmigiano. His was made from the milk of a special herd of red-haired Italian cattle.

Another dish, the traditional pairing of potato and salt cod (think brandade), was reimagined this way: boil, peel, and freeze-dry purple-fleshed Peruvian potatoes, then grind into a very bright violet powder. Slowly simmer a slice of salt cod in olive oil. Make a smear of yellow garlic sauce on a giant white plate. Roll the warm salt cod in the purple potato powder and place it on the plate. Garnish with violets!

A Danish chef loved the earth and its seasons. For his dish of winter root vegetables, he cooked turnips, radishes, and carrots in butter. Then he made some fake earth with edible ingredients, advising that it should look dark and loose like rich mulch, but warning that its flavor should not overpower the vegetables. He heaped a good shovelful of the "dirt" onto a large slab of slate and laid the cooked root vegetables on top. He placed a dome over the vegetables and piped in a large blast of wood smoke. Presentation? Remove the dome and the dish is smoking, steaming, and earthy.

A very well known English chef showed photographs of his creations. A signature dish is a raw shellfish salad scattered over faux sand and garnished with seaweed. This salad is accompanied by an iPod, hidden in a large seashell and loaded with sea sounds.

Saved for last was the famous Spaniard who has inspired so many imitators and pretenders (and whom, surprisingly, I liked best of all). He was an extraordinary gentleman, completely down-to-earth and engaging. He told us it doesn't matter what you cook, what your ingredients are, or where you live, as long as you have soul. He seemed to genuinely enjoy his inventions. Some of his dishes were as simple as grapefruit sections, slightly dried to concentrate their centers. Others involved freezing fresh tomato juice in the shape of a balloon.

It was all quite entertaining. But afterward, when I got back to Paris and thought about what I wanted to cook for friends the following night at home, I craved real vegetables and a plain roast. Though perhaps I would splurge on baby spring lamb from the Pyrenees—the butcher had told me it was available. Something simple. With absolutely no foam.

Asparagus-Scrambled Eggs

The French often begin a meal with soft scrambled eggs, *oeufs brouillés*. (In its ultimate rendition, the eggs are scrambled with black truffles.) But I actually discovered this dish in Spain, where it was made with wild asparagus. I love the combination of the bite of asparagus with the soft egg. Use skinny asparagus, or wild if you can find them. Cook this just before you sit down to eat: it'll be ready in minutes.

2 pounds asparagus
4 tablespoons butter
1 garlic clove, finely chopped
Salt and pepper

8 eggs, beaten
Several sprigs of mint and basil,
  leaves chopped

{CONTINUED}

Snap off the tough ends of the asparagus. Cut the stalks into 1-inch lengths; if your asparagus are thick, halve the stalks lengthwise before cutting them. In a large skillet, heat 2 tablespoons of the butter over medium heat. Add the asparagus and chopped garlic, season with salt and pepper, and cook until just done, about 2 minutes.

Remove the asparagus from the skillet and set aside. Heat the remaining butter in the same pan. Season the eggs with salt and pepper and add them to the pan. Stir gently until the eggs are barely set.

Fold in the asparagus, then spoon onto a warmed platter. Scatter chopped mint and basil on top.

Fork-Mashed Potatoes

In France these are called *pommes de terres à la fourchette,* which sounds glamorous for a dish of humble home-style potatoes mashed with a fork. You can make them as smooth as you like, or keep them rough and chunky.

2½ pounds yellow-fleshed potatoes, such as Yukon Gold	½ cup milk or cream
	¼ cup olive oil
Salt and pepper	2 tablespoons butter

Peel and cube the potatoes. Boil them in salted water 12 to 15 minutes, until fork-tender. Drain the potatoes and return them to the pot. Season with salt and pepper. Heat the milk in a small saucepan until just under a boil.

Pour the hot milk over the potatoes and add the olive oil and butter. Use a large fork to mash the potatoes to the consistency you like, then transfer to a warm serving bowl.

Spring Lamb with Rosemary

In Spain and Italy, tender, milk-fed baby lamb is well-known and appreciated, and the best French butchers carry tiny *agneau du lait* from the Pyrenees. Here in the States, lamb that small is hard to find, but some small farms now market midsize spring lamb. The rack of lamb is the tenderest cut of the beast and the easiest to cook. Ask your butcher for the smallest racks. SERVES 4 TO 6

Two 8-bone racks of lamb,
  frenched
Salt and pepper
2 garlic cloves, smashed to a paste
  with a little salt

Several sprigs of rosemary,
  leaves coarsely chopped
Olive oil

Season the racks liberally with salt and pepper. With your hands, rub each rack with the garlic and chopped rosemary and a drizzle of olive oil. Place the racks fat side up in a roasting pan and leave them at room temperature for an hour or so.

Preheat the oven to 400°F. Roast the lamb for about 20 minutes, until the racks are nicely browned, with an interior temperature of 125°F on an instant-read thermometer. Remove from the oven, cover loosely with foil, and let rest for about 10 minutes. Put a serving platter in the oven to warm.

Transfer the racks to a carving board and slice between the bones. Arrange the little chops on the platter and serve.

Dandelion Greens Salad

The tender leaves of spring dandelions make a wonderful salad. Cultivated varieties of dandelion are usually less bitter than wild. In any case, look for the smallest leaves. The larger broad-leafed variety that you often find in the market is better wilted. If you can't find dandelion greens, you can make this salad with curly endive or watercress.

1 shallot, finely diced

2 to 3 tablespoons red wine
  vinegar

Salt and pepper

1 garlic clove, smashed to a paste
  with a little salt

1 teaspoon Dijon mustard

¼ cup olive oil

4 large handfuls dandelion
  greens, about 1 pound

Macerate the shallot in the red wine vinegar with a pinch of salt for 5 minutes. Add the garlic, mustard, and pepper, then stir in the olive oil. Taste and adjust the seasonings.

Put the dandelion greens in a large salad bowl, and sprinkle lightly with salt. Add half the dressing and toss. Taste and add a little more dressing if you think it's necessary.

Strawberries with Sugar and Cream

The quality of both the berries and the cream really matters here. Giant supermarket strawberries are sure to disappoint, so head for the farm stand or the farmers' market. You want berries that are deep red, with fresh, bright green leaves and stems. You should be able to smell them before you see them! Use homemade crème fraîche or the best commercial crème fraîche you can find; or use organic cream (avoid ultrapasteurized cream). Use whatever sugar you prefer. I grew up eating strawberries with brown sugar.

2 to 3 pints perfect organic   Sugar
    strawberries
1 pint Crème Fraîche (recipe follows)
    or heavy cream, lightly whipped

Rinse the berries quickly in cool water, drain well on a kitchen towel, and gently pile them onto a platter. Pass small bowls of the crème fraîche and sugar. Eat the strawberries with your fingers, dipping them first in the sugar and then in the cream—or vice versa.

Crème Fraîche

Heat 2 cups organic heavy cream, not ultrapasteurized, to just under a boil. Cool to room temperature. Stir in ¼ cup plain yogurt or buttermilk. Transfer to a glass, ceramic, or strainless steel bowl and cover with a clean towel. Leave at room temperature for about 12 hours, until slightly thickened. For a tarter flavor, let it stand for 24 hours. Cover well and store, refrigerated, for up to 2 weeks.

Reclaiming Arugula

Fennel Soup with a Green Swirl
Pork Scaloppine with Lemon, Capers, and Chopped Arugula
Zucchini Pancakes
Italian Spice Cake
Tangerines

"Oh, arugula!" an Italian friend of mine exclaimed
recently. "It is so-o-o tiresome!" I was surprised. "I thought all Italians liked
it?" "Yes, I like it," she said. "It's just that you can't go anywhere anymore
without finding arugula on everything: pizzas, salads, carpaccio, tagliata.
They've ruined it for me!"

She had a point. Arugula, once unknown here and now ubiquitous,
has become synonymous with elitism and effeteism—a snob's green. It's a
funny thing to happen to leaves that are fed to rabbits all across Europe.

But wait. Sharp, nutty, slightly spicy arugula is truly a wonderful
green. Just a few leaves can pick up any salad. Use it instead of basil for
a good pesto over pasta with anchovies. Or wilt it, like spinach, in a sauté
of zucchini. Best of all, perhaps, is the simple arugula salad, the leaves
chopped and dressed with lemon and olive oil, the way it's done in Milano.

There are all kinds of arugula. Tiny, tender young shoots; medium-
sized "salad" arugula; the large-leafed spinach-like variety you find in

New York City; and the small, skinny, reticulated "wild" arugula that's suddenly showing up in good markets everywhere. Botanically, arugula is a brassica called *Eruca sativa,* which means it's related to cabbage, mustard, and broccoli—no surprise there. In Italy, it's called *rucola* (among other names); arugula is an Americanization of the Italian word. In France, it is called *roquette* (or *ricchetti,* in the South of France). And almost no one uses its English name "rocket," as it's listed in *The Oxford Companion to Italian Food,* with this understatement: "The current overuse of whole rocket leaves as garnish is not as satisfactory as the many unpretentious recipes in which it is added, chopped, to sauces and cooked dishes." My point exactly.

Fennel Soup with a Green Swirl

Make sure you find the freshest, brightest, most fragrant fennel for this soup. Fennel should be firm, shiny, and pale green. Don't buy fennel that looks withered or brown or stringy. Check the root ends of the bulbs to make sure they've been freshly cut. And, since you'll use the fronds for the pureed swirl, it's important that they be green, feathery, and abundant.

FOR THE SOUP

¼ cup olive oil

3 medium fennel bulbs, trimmed
  and sliced

1 large onion, sliced

4 garlic cloves, chopped

Salt and pepper

¼ cup long-grain white rice

6 cups chicken broth or water, or
  as needed

FOR THE SWIRL

1 cup roughly chopped fennel
  fronds

½ cup parsley leaves

½ cup basil leaves

¼ cup chopped scallions

½ cup olive oil

Salt and pepper

In a large heavy-bottomed pot, heat the olive oil over medium heat. Add the sliced fennel, onion, and garlic. Season generously with salt and pepper, and stew the vegetables, stirring every few minutes, until they are softened and lightly colored.

Add the rice and broth or water. Bring to a boil, then lower the heat to a gentle simmer. Taste the broth, add more seasoning if necessary, and simmer for 20 minutes.

Puree the soup in a blender, then pass through a fine-mesh strainer to remove any fibrous strands. Return the strained soup to the pot. Check the consistency. If it's too thick, add a bit of water or broth.

Rinse and dry the blender, and put all the ingredients for the swirl into the blender at once. Blend on high speed until you have a smooth green puree. Transfer to a small bowl.

To serve, reheat the soup and ladle it into soup bowls. Swirl a tablespoon of the green puree into each bowl.

Pork Scaloppine with Lemon, Capers, and Chopped Arugula

We're talking here about thinly sliced (but not pounded) pork cut from the lean end of a pork loin. Ask your butcher to cut the slices for you. It will cook quickly and stay tender. It is still difficult to find good veal these days, but better pork is happening all across the country, which is why I use it here instead of the traditional veal. SERVES 4 TO 6

12 thin (about ⅜-inch-thick) slices
   pork cut from the loin
Salt and pepper
About ½ cup olive oil
2 tablespoons roughly chopped
   parsley

2 teaspoons grated lemon zest
1 tablespoon capers, rinsed and
   roughly chopped
2 garlic cloves, finely chopped
½ pound arugula, chopped
Lemon wedges

Season both sides of the pork slices with salt and pepper and drizzle with olive oil. Heat two cast-iron skillets over medium-high heat. When the pans are hot, lay 6 slices of pork in each pan and let them cook for about 2 minutes, until nicely browned. Turn and cook for 2 minutes on the other side. Remove the scaloppine to a warm serving platter.

In one of the pans, heat 2 tablespoons of olive oil over medium heat. Add the parsley, lemon zest, capers, and garlic and let sizzle for a bare minute. Spoon the sauce over the scaloppine and top each slice with a handful of chopped arugula. Garnish the platter with lemon wedges.

Zucchini Pancakes

These light little zucchini cakes are simply grated zucchini bound with egg and a little flour. To me they taste quintessentially Italian, sort of like a zucchini frittata, especially if you add the Parmigiano. They're also delicious at room temperature, which makes them perfect for a picnic or a lunch box.

8 to 10 small zucchini, about
   3 pounds
2 teaspoons salt
2 eggs
½ teaspoon pepper

1 bunch scallions, finely chopped
3 tablespoons all-purpose flour
½ cup finely grated Parmigiano
   (optional)
Olive oil for frying

Grate the zucchini on the medium holes of a box grater. Toss the grated zucchini with the salt and let it drain in a colander for about 20 minutes. Squeeze very dry in a clean kitchen towel.

In a large mixing bowl, beat the eggs with the pepper and scallions. Add the flour, then add the grated zucchini and cheese, if using, and mix thoroughly.

Pour olive oil into a cast-iron skillet to a depth of ¼ inch and heat. Carefully place spoonfuls of the zucchini mixture in the pan, then flatten them to a diameter of about 2 inches. Make only a few pancakes at a time so you don't crowd them, and turn each one once, letting them cook for about 3 to 4 minutes on each side, until golden. The heat should stay at moderate; if you get impatient and try to cook them too rapidly over high heat, they'll get too dark too quickly, and you don't want that.

Serve immediately, or hold in a warm oven until the entire batch is cooked.

Italian Spice Cake

This is a dense spice cake that, like panforte, keeps well. Try to wait until the next day to eat it, in small, thin slices. A bowl of tangerines makes a perfect accompaniment.

½ cup sugar

½ cup water

¼ cup honey

1 teaspoon grated orange zest

1 teaspoon grated lemon zest

½ teaspoon coarsely ground
   black pepper

A little grated nutmeg

Pinch of cayenne

¼ teaspoon ground cloves

¼ teaspoon ground allspice

½ teaspoon ground cinnamon

1 tablespoon unsweetened cocoa
   powder

2 eggs, beaten

½ cup golden raisins

1 cup natural (unblanched)
   whole almonds

1 cup all-purpose flour

½ cup almond flour

Preheat the oven to 375°F. Butter and flour a 9-inch tart pan; set aside. In a large saucepan, dissolve the sugar in the water and honey and simmer for a couple of minutes.

Remove from the heat and add the citrus zests, the spices, and the cocoa. Add the eggs and mix well. Stir in the raisins and almonds, then gradually stir in the flours.

Pour the batter into the pan and bake the cake for 35 to 40 minutes, until a knife inserted into the cake comes out dry. Unmold after about 10 minutes and cool on a rack.

In a Sicilian Kitchen

Sicilian Salad
Pasta "Timballo" with Fresh Ricotta
Fried Puffs with Honey (Sfince)

Sicily may be part of Italy, but it really feels like another country altogether. Palermo is crazy! Mountain-like rocky promontories hover over the coastline with castles on their peaks, and little villages climb their slopes. There are ancient caves, and giant wind turbines, sleek and white and modern, their slim blades turning busily. Along the highway, factories and oil tanks stand cheek by jowl with ruins of old stone farmhouses, shabby high-rise apartments, and grand walled villas. Blackened Victorian structures and ornate government palazzi are interspersed with used-car lots. Vacation houses clog every square meter of waterfront; tall cranes hover and bulldozers abound. A billboard advertises a new kind of electric bicycle—*Spina e via,* it implores: plug it in and go! But everyone is going already . . . cars, trucks of every size, scooters, motorcycles, all headed in every direction in a hurry, weaving between what would be lanes if there were any painted stripes.

But there's another side to Sicily and that's where we're headed. We've come to visit Fabrizia Lanza at her family's estate, the winery Regaleali, about an hour's drive from Palermo. We gladly leave the urban chaos behind as we head inland, traversing the twisted roads past low stone walls, vineyards, and orange groves. Everywhere are flowering fruit trees, patches of wild fennel, jumbles of cactus, stretches of pasture, and rolling green hills. It's spring, but the distant mountains are still snow-topped.

Fabrizia, the daughter of the renowned cook Anna Tasca Lanza, is taking over her mother's cooking school (Anna is retiring after twenty years and four seminal cookbooks). Regaleali, it turns out, is more than the grounds of the estate. The family owns the valley as far as the eye can see: grapevines and olive trees, a small herd of *testa rossa* sheep, a few vegetable gardens, a little family chapel, two large stone villas, and a scattering of outbuildings. It could be another century but for the automobiles, tractors, and stainless steel wine tanks.

Fabrizia shares with her mother a love of the Sicilian countryside, its history, and traditional cuisine. Sicily, ruled at various times by the Normans, Arabs, Spanish, and French, has taken rich culinary influences from its conquerors. Indeed, the cooking of each village differs from the next. In Trapani, for example, on the northwest coast, the local specialty is couscous (we are African, they told me there); on the opposite end of the island, in Etna, no one makes couscous. Fabrizia, who clearly loves to cook and to share her knowledge in equal measure, has been working on documenting the vanishing traditional cuisine, interviewing and recording the stories of the old ladies from nearby villages as they demonstrate, for instance, the traditional breads for the feast of San Giuseppe, St. Joseph's Day.

We spend a few days cooking together and Fabrizia teaches me several dishes from her vast repertoire. These are simple dishes, most with ingredients plucked straight from the garden. In her Sicilian kitchen we become fast friends.

Mercato Ballarò, Palermo's popular street market, is souk-like and plenty old, winding and spilling among narrow streets and alleys, lively and beautiful, twisting and shouting.

We are told we must visit the stand of Joise, whose specialty is *quarume.* When we order a little plate of it, Joise mimes the parts of veal we'll be eating. Clutching his breast, tapping his head, holding his stomach, and pointing to his shoes, he says, *"Mammalia, testa, trippa, piedo."* We approve heartily of this boiled antipasto he slices cold, to be eaten with salt and lemon. But we have come to sample his tripe specialties, and for this we are beckoned inside the little dining area to two old tables with marble tops (one marked "nonsmoking"). We are given paper napkins, silverware, a small loaf of bread, and a liter of wine. There are two tripe dishes on the menu, and Joise gives us both: one simply boiled with a bit of meat, *nervetti,* and ventricles and served in its broth. The other is simmered with tomato, thickened with bread crumbs, and sprinkled generously with aged pecorino. *Buonissimo!*

We leave and venture into the market, as cacophonous as Palermo itself. There we see all manner of fish, calamari, clams, anchovies, *bottarga di tonno.* Barrels of olives and capers in salt. Masses of lemons and oranges, always with leaves. Forests of freshly cut artichokes, mountains of cauliflower (the local, green-fleshed sort). Stacks of ricotta—fresh, smoked, and baked. Young pecorino with red pepper or black. Piles of spices. Baskets of garlic and pink-tinged spring onions. Bundles of fresh herbs. Pyramids of greens. Jars and jars of deepest red *estratto di pomodoro,* sun-dried tomato paste. Coils of sausage, pillars of prosciutto and pancetta.

There's a guy selling *sfincione,* the Sicilian pizza. Someone else is frying *panelle,* crisp fritters made from *farina di ceci,* chickpea flour. And there's *ca'meusa,* a local favorite, boiled spleen on a bun. And *arancini,* fried rice balls, and *gelato,* always in a brioche to eat on the run—surely the original ice cream sandwich. That settles it, I tell myself. I'm moving to Sicily.

Sicilian Salad

In Sicily, the citrus is so phenomenal even the lemons taste better, somehow more delicious and round. We devised a simple salad—lettuces freshly picked, crisply fresh sliced fennel, young radishes, wild garlic, brown-leafed catmint, fruity olive oil, lemon juice, and orange slices. I said, "This salad tastes like Sicily. I'll call it Sicilian Salad." Fabrizia laughed and replied, "No Sicilian would ever eat it!" In Sicily, the preference is for cooked vegetables, not raw.

1 fennel bulb, trimmed

Salt and pepper

Juice of ½ lemon

1 garlic clove, smashed to a paste
   with a little salt

3 tablespoons olive oil

1 small bunch radishes, thinly
   sliced

2 scallions, thinly sliced

2 heads fresh-picked tender
   lettuce, torn into large pieces

A large handful of arugula

2 navel oranges, peeled and sliced
   into rings

A few mint leaves, chopped

Thinly slice the fennel and put it in a salad bowl. Season with salt and pepper. Whisk together the lemon juice, garlic, and olive oil and pour it over the fennel. Add the radishes, scallions, and greens, sprinkle lightly with salt, and toss gently with your hands to coat the leaves. Put the orange slices on top of the salad and scatter the chopped mint over all.

HONEST RICOTTA

At Regaleali, they milk their small herd of sheep twice a day. Three kinds of cheese are made in an old-fashioned traditional cheese kitchen, where the milk is heated in a copper cauldron set over a wood fire. When it clabbers, the milk is drained into baskets to make *tuma,* fresh curd cheese. The *tuma* firms in the baskets overnight and then is salted to make *primo sale,* fresh pecorino; or it's aged with peppercorns for the hard, tangy *pecorino stagioanato.* Fresh ricotta (*ricotta* means cooked twice) is made in the same copper cauldron from the reserved whey drained from the curds. The watery whey is simmered gently for about 20 minutes, until the remaining milk solids almost miraculously coagulate, then the solids are gently salted and spooned into baskets to drain. When you taste it, this ricotta is the best thing you have ever eaten. In Fabrizia's kitchen, we mixed the fresh ricotta with tomato sauce for a pasta; stuffed fried cannoli shells with ricotta cream; and made a sweetened ricotta cake called *cassata alla siciliana.* For breakfast we ate warm ricotta with honey.

Pasta "Timballo" with Fresh Ricotta

A timballo is a classic Sicilian pasta dish reserved for formal occasions. Baked in a deep pan and covered with bread crumbs, flaky pastry, or slices of eggplant, it is impressive: when the timballo is unmolded and arrives at the table, it has the grand presence of a birthday cake. Even a simplified version of the timballo, such as the one that follows, with the pasta piled on a huge platter, is thrilling. And equally tasty.

The dish is made with *anelli,* a dried ring-shaped pasta made from hard wheat. SERVES 4 TO 6

1 pound anelli pasta
Olive oil
Salt and pepper
Red pepper flakes
4 cups Tomato Sauce
  (recipe follows)

1 pound best-quality fresh ricotta,
  at room temperature
Grated pecorino
A handful of basil leaves,
  roughly chopped

Bring a big pot of salted water to a boil. Preheat the oven to 350°F. Boil the pasta for 12 or 15 minutes; it should be barely al dente. Drain the pasta and put it in a large bowl. Drizzle with a little fruity olive oil, and season to taste with salt, black pepper, and red pepper flakes.

Meanwhile, heat the tomato sauce. Have a large, deep ovenproof platter ready.

Spoon about half the sauce into the platter and stir half of the ricotta into the sauce, leaving it rather lumpy. Pile the pasta on the sauce on the platter, and spoon the rest of the sauce on top of the pasta. Top with spoonfuls of the remaining ricotta and sprinkle with grated pecorino. Put the platter in the oven for about 10 minutes, to heat through completely.

Sprinkle with the basil, and serve more pecorino on the side.

Tomato Sauce

Although tomatoes reached Italy only five hundred years ago, Italian—and especially Sicilian—cuisine is unthinkable without them. *Conserva,* home-made tomato sauce, and *estratto di pomodoro,* sun-dried tomato paste, are used almost daily in the Sicilian kitchen. Ideally you would have made this sauce in tomato season. MAKES ABOUT 8 CUPS

¼ cup olive oil
1 large yellow onion, finely diced
6 garlic cloves, chopped
Salt and pepper

8 pounds ripe tomatoes, peeled,
    seeded, and chopped
A sprig of basil

Heat the olive oil in a large heavy-bottomed pot. Sauté the onion over medium heat until quite soft but not browned, about 10 minutes. Add the garlic, salt, and pepper and let cook for a minute or two. Add the tomatoes and basil, bring to a boil, and let the sauce bubble briskly for about 5 minutes.

Reduce the heat to quite low and cook slowly for 1 to 1½ hours, stirring frequently to make sure the tomatoes don't stick or burn. The sauce is done when the volume of tomatoes is reduced by almost half and the sauce has a nice consistency—not too thick and not too thin.

Can or freeze the sauce to use throughout the year.

Fried Puffs with Honey (Sfince)

Made to celebrate St. Joseph's Day, these fried puffs of dough reflect the Arab influence on Sicilian cuisine. Sometimes they can be a little stodgy and doughy, but Fabrizia makes a lighter version with French pâte à choux (cream puff dough), which I think is a very good idea. You can make the dough a few hours ahead, but *sfince* are best eaten quickly once they are fried.

6 tablespoons butter

Pinch of salt

1 teaspoon sugar

1 cup water

1 cup all-purpose flour

4 eggs

Vegetable oil for frying

Warmed honey for drizzling

In a heavy-bottomed saucepan, combine the butter, salt, sugar, and water and bring to a boil over medium-high heat. Add the flour all at once, stirring madly with a wooden spoon until the mixture forms a ball. This will happen quickly, in about a minute.

Transfer the hot dough to a mixing bowl and, with an electric mixer, beat in the eggs one at a time. Then beat for a couple of minutes, until the eggs are well incorporated and the mixture is shiny. What you're making is a very thick batter.

Proceed to fry the *sfince* right away, or leave the dough at room temperature until you're ready to fry them, for up to 2 hours.

Heat 2 inches of oil in a wide deep skillet until it reaches 375°F on a deep-fry thermometer. Using a teaspoon, make little blobs of dough and put them carefully into the oil. Do this in batches, frying only 8 or 10 puffs at a time so you don't crowd the pan. The *sfince* will puff up immediately, but you have to nurse them and turn them over so that they cook evenly. Fry until golden brown, about 5 minutes. Lift the puffs from the oil with a slotted spoon and drain on paper towels. When all the puffs are fried, transfer to a platter and drizzle lightly with warmed honey.

The Flavor of Smoke

Scallion Broth
Tea-Smoked-Chicken Salad with Ginger Vinaigrette
Sesame Peanut Candy

Once upon a time, before factory farming, chicken was a luxury, signifying prosperity—a treat that marked special occasions. And it tasted like something. In nearly every culture, chicken had iconic significance, and, in many, it still does. The smell of chicken roasting, boiling, or simmering always conjures a sense memory for me. Perhaps I inherited it. My great-grandmother, a tough bird herself (or so the story goes) was a professional chicken wrangler. She had a stand in the market selling live chickens in Dayton, Ohio, much to the horror of her twin granddaughters, little Marjory and Dorothy. But she was from the old country, and it didn't bother her a bit to take a chicken by the legs from a wooden crate, slit its throat, quickly pluck the feathers, and remove the guts. And if gutting an old hen happened to reveal an unborn egg or two, so much the better. People paid a bit more for these shell-less delicacies, so good in a bowl of chicken soup. She didn't get rich in the process, but she eked out a living, and there was usually chicken for the family.

In those days, every little mom-and-pop farm in America would have, in addition to a chicken coop, a few guinea hens in the yard. You didn't

really have to care for them because they like to perch high, in the eaves of a barn or the branches of a tree. They made good "watchbirds" because, like geese, their habit is to scream, loud and often. It's a pity that more people don't know about guinea hens, because if you are at all an aficionado of roast chicken, you're sure to be thrilled by the flavor of roast guinea hen.

There is one farm that raises guinea fowl, run by French people, in northern California. The French love their *pintades* and the Italians, their *faraona.* In Europe, guinea fowl are even cheaper than chicken. These birds have goodness bred into them. I think of them as the über-chicken, because they have so much flavor, but they are actually related to pheasants. You wouldn't call their flavor gamey, but you would call it deep. A little garlic, rosemary, salt, and pepper are all you need for a true feast.

As long as we're talking about tasty birds, let's not forget the duck (Chinese roast duck; rare-grilled duck breast in the French manner!), nor the quail (and quail eggs!), best nibbled with the fingers. But especially, let's toast the young farm-raised pigeon—or squab, if you're squeamish. Squab has the most divine flavor of any bird, and that goes double for squab liver.

I once moved into a house in the country near Pecos, New Mexico, with an abandoned pigeon coop in the back. By coincidence, one day some Texan friends came to visit with a cage full of live pigeons. By the time dinner was over, they had persuaded me to install a dozen pigeons in the old coop.

The pigeons did what pigeons do, and soon began laying eggs, always two at a time. In a few weeks I had about four dozen young squabs. Then one afternoon I did what cooks do: I killed them all, then sat in the grass and plucked them. There's a photo of me somewhere wearing a big smile and a lot of feathers. I invited a big group of friends to a pigeon feed. I braised the legs, grilled the breasts, and made pâté from the livers.

I thought of my great-grandmother, the chicken lady, and wondered what she would think of her great-grandson, plucking pigeons in Pecos.

Scallion Broth

You need to simmer the chicken legs before you smoke them for the chicken salad in this menu. In the process, you obtain a tasty light broth to serve as its own course or, even better, in a little bowl along with the salad.

6 chicken legs

Salt and pepper

8 cups water

One 1-inch piece ginger, peeled
  and sliced

2 garlic cloves, sliced

4 scallions, roughly chopped, plus
  2 tablespoons slivered scallions
  for garnish

3 star anise

Season the chicken legs generously with salt and pepper. (You can do this a couple of hours ahead, or even the night before, and refrigerate them.) Put the chicken legs in a heavy-bottomed pot and cover with the water. Add the sliced ginger, garlic, roughly chopped scallions, and star anise. Bring to a boil, then turn down to a gentle simmer. Check the legs at 30 minutes.

When they're done, remove them and set aside for the salad. Simmer the broth for another 30 minutes.

Strain the broth, skim off any fat, and check the seasoning. The seasoned chicken legs will have added their salt and pepper to the broth, but it might need a little salt. Refrigerate the broth until you're ready to use it, for up to 2 days.

To serve, reheat the broth, pour it into small bowls, and garnish with the slivered scallions.

Tea-Smoked-Chicken Salad with Ginger Vinaigrette

The Chinese technique of tea-smoking is utterly simple, but the results are complex and delicious. No other smoking smells like tea-smoking or gives food that signature slightly glazed look. Many kinds of salad greens will work here, from watercress to curly endive to tender mustard greens, or even young spinach. SERVES 4 TO 6

½ cup black tea leaves

½ cup raw white rice

½ cup packed brown sugar

2 or 3 star anise, crushed

1 tablespoon black peppercorns

1 teaspoon fennel seeds

1 teaspoon whole cloves

6 cooked chicken legs from the
     previous recipe

12 quail eggs

4 to 6 handfuls salad greens

Salt and pepper

Ginger Vinaigrette
     (recipe follows)

To smoke the chicken, you need a closed pot such as a Dutch oven or a roasting pan with a lid. Line the bottom of the pot with foil. Mix the tea, rice, sugar, and aromatics in a bowl, then spread the mixture right on the foil. You will need a little rack above it for the chicken. Put the chicken legs in one layer on the rack, then put on the lid.

Preheat the oven to 400°F. Put the pot on the stove over high heat. Now you will have to depend upon your ear and your nose to tell you what's going on, because you can't peek, or you'll lose the smoke. What you'll hear is the sugar beginning to crackle, and you'll smell the tea and aromatics beginning to smoke. Leave over high heat for about 2 minutes, then turn off the heat.

Put the pan in the oven and roast for about 10 minutes. This should be sufficient to give the chicken the traditional tea-smoked flavor. It's best to

take the pot outdoors before you open it so you don't fill your kitchen with smoke. In any case, it is important to release the smoke somehow, near a vent or an open window, for example. Open the pot and remove the legs to a platter. Set the platter aside and let the chicken cool to room temperature. The burnt remains of the tea and sugar will be there on the foil, waiting to be thrown away.

To cook the quail eggs, bring a small pot of water to a rolling boil. Put in the quail eggs and keep the water boiling for a minute and a half. Immediately remove them and submerge the eggs in a bowl of ice water. This gives you the kind of boiled egg I like, hard-cooked with a soft center.

To assemble the salad, put the greens in a big bowl and lightly salt and pepper them. Add 2 tablespoons of the vinaigrette, just enough to coat the leaves. Toss the leaves gently, and divide among 4 to 6 plates.

Place each chicken leg in its own little nest of greens, or, if you'd rather, shred the chicken. I like to garnish the plates with the quail eggs in their shells, but if you prefer, you can peel them. Drizzle a little vinaigrette over the chicken and serve.

OTHER BIRDS TO SMOKE

Quail, guinea hens, game hens, and duck legs are also excellent candidates for tea-smoking, simmered first as in the recipe on page 71. I've also smoked rare pan-seared duck breasts and rare roasted squab with excellent results.

Ginger Vinaigrette

1 shallot, finely diced

1 garlic clove, smashed to a paste
   with a little salt

1 tablespoon white wine vinegar
   or rice vinegar

Salt and pepper

2 teaspoons finely diced or grated
   peeled ginger

1 tablespoon Dijon mustard

¼ cup grapeseed or other
   mild vegetable oil

1 teaspoon toasted sesame oil

Juice of ½ lime

Combine the shallot and garlic in a small bowl with the vinegar. Add a little salt and pepper and let sit for about 5 minutes, then whisk in all the remaining ingredients. MAKES ABOUT ½ CUP

Sesame Peanut Candy

These candies are a heavenly cross between meringue and nougat. You can make them a day or two ahead and store in an airtight container.

2 cups raw peanuts
½ cup sesame seeds
1 cup brown sugar

½ teaspoon salt
2 egg whites

Preheat the oven to 350°F. Line a baking sheet with parchment paper. Mix the peanuts, sesame seeds, sugar, and salt in a mixing bowl. Whisk the egg whites into soft peaks. Stir half the whites into the nut mixture, then gently fold in the remaining whites.

Spread evenly on the baking sheet about ½ inch thick. Bake until the brittle turns a toasty brown, about 25 minutes. Cool on a rack.

Peel off the parchment paper while the brittle is still a bit warm.

Allow to cool and harden completely before cutting into small squares.

Feeling Vietnamese

Vegetable Rice Paper Rolls
Pho (Vietnamese Beef Soup)
Black Sticky Rice Pudding with Coconut Cream

Though I'd often eaten Vietnamese food in California, oddly, it took a bowl of soup in Paris to hook me. After shopping the early morning market at the Place Maubert, we discovered a noodle shop nearby. It happened to be one of those damp, chill spring days the French specialize in, so we sat outside on the sidewalk terrace across from the busy market to seek warmth in a big, brothy bowl of pho. The name is pronounced "feu," like the French word for fire, and some people claim it betrays the French influence on Vietnamese cuisine; others cite a much older relationship to other Chinese and Japanese noodle soups. No matter—it's delicious. There are other offerings on the menu, but I always opt for the pho, its fragrant broth layered with fresh herbs, rice noodles, bean sprouts, and sharp hot chiles. We usually start with two other favorites: crispy fried egg rolls (known in France as *nems*) and vegetable rolls, which are called *rouleaux du printemps* ("spring rolls"). These are served with a pile of sweet herbs and lettuce leaves. The earthy yet surprisingly delicate ingredients and fresh combinations of Vietnamese cooking always taste healthy, clean, and restorative.

Vegetable Rice Paper Rolls

Easy to assemble, these fresh, savory rolls can be a light appetizer on their own, or you can make a platter of them to accompany the soup. Vegetable rolls are typically a little bland, but I like to make a well-seasoned filling sparked with ginger. Sometimes called rice paper, the wrappers are basically disc-shaped dry noodles made from rice flour. I keep a package of them on hand in the pantry. MAKES 8 ROLLS

1 small cucumber, peeled and cut
    into long julienne
1 medium carrot, peeled and cut
    into long julienne
2 scallions, finely sliced
One 1-inch piece ginger, peeled
    and shredded
1 serrano chile, finely diced
Salt and pepper
¼ teaspoon toasted sesame oil

8 large rice paper wrappers
Basil leaves
Mint leaves
Cilantro sprigs
1 firm-ripe avocado, cut into
    8 wedges
Lettuce leaves and herb sprigs for
    garnish
Dipping Sauce (recipe follows)

Put the cucumber, carrot, scallions, ginger, and chile in a bowl. Season lightly with salt and pepper. Add the sesame oil and toss lightly.

To prepare the rolls, have a bowl of hot water near your work surface. Dip a wrapper in hot water until it wilts and becomes translucent, only about 15 seconds. Lift the wrapper from the water and lay it on a cutting board. Place a few basil leaves, mint leaves, and cilantro sprigs on the bottom half of the wrapper. Then spoon on a small amount of the cucumber/carrot mixture, and top with a wedge of avocado. Fold over the sides of the wrapper slightly, then roll it into a firm cigar shape. Set aside. As the roll cools, the color will return to rice white. Repeat with the other wrappers.

For a platter of rolls, cut each one in half. Serve with lettuce leaves, herb sprigs, and the dipping sauce. It's traditional to wrap each portion in a lettuce leaf with herb sprigs before dunking it in the dipping sauce.

Dipping Sauce

½ cup rice vinegar

2 tablespoons brown sugar or
  crushed palm sugar

2 tablespoons fish sauce

2 tablespoons chopped scallions

Juice of 1 lime

1 serrano or Asian chile, finely
  slivered (optional)

Mix all the ingredients together well in a small bowl. If you like your sauce spicier, add a little chopped fresh chile. Serve with the vegetable rolls.

Pho (Vietnamese Beef Soup)

In Vietnam, pho is street food, basic, hearty, and filling, sold from a cart with a few little stools in front. Here, you can get pho at little bare-bones sit-down restaurants, where you crowd in for a quick lunch. Platters of mint and basil leaves are stacked up and ready, because they are constantly needed. At such places, there is a rich and long menu of variations, pho with meatballs or tripe, for example. Pho fanatics customize their bowls with all kinds of extras and peculiarities. So you'll want to develop your own house pho.

Classically the soup is finished with thinly sliced raw beef that cooks quickly in the soup, but your pho can be any combination that pleases you.

The broth is the essence of the soup, so it's important to take great care with it. It's not difficult, but it makes all the difference between a pho that sings and one that just sits there.

FOR THE SOUP

1½ pounds short ribs

1½ pounds oxtails or beef shank

1 large onion, halved

One 3-inch piece unpeeled ginger, thickly sliced

6 quarts water

1 star anise

1 small piece cinnamon stick

½ teaspoon coriander seeds

½ teaspoon fennel seeds

¼ teaspoon whole cloves

6 cardamom pods

2 tablespoons soy sauce

1 tablespoon fish sauce

2 teaspoons sugar

Salt and pepper

1 pound dried rice noodles

½ pound fresh bean sprouts

1 sweet red onion, thinly sliced

FOR THE GARNISH

Mint sprigs

Cilantro sprigs

Basil sprigs

6 scallions, slivered

2 serrano or 6 small Asian chiles, finely slivered

Lime wedges

Bring a large pot of water to a boil. Put in the short ribs and oxtails and boil for 10 minutes, then drain and discard the water. This preliminary boiling makes a cleaner-tasting broth.

Set a heavy-bottomed soup pot over medium-high heat, add the onion, cut side down, and ginger, and lightly char for about 10 minutes, until the halves are charred but not quite burnt. Add the short ribs, oxtails, and the 6 quarts of water and bring to a hard boil, then turn down to a simmer. Add the star anise, cinnamon stick, coriander and fennel seeds, cloves, and cardamom. Then add the soy sauce, fish sauce, sugar, and salt and pepper and let simmer, uncovered. From time to time, skim off rising foam, fat, and debris.

After an hour or so, check the tenderness of the meat. It will probably take an hour and a half for the meat to get really fork-tender.

When the meat is done, remove it from the pot, take the meat off the bones, and reserve. Put the bones back in the pot to simmer in the broth for about another hour and a half.

When the broth is done, taste it for salt and add more if necessary. Strain it through a fine-mesh strainer. Chop the cooked meat and add it to the broth. Cool and refrigerate. (The broth can be made a day ahead.)

When you're ready to serve the pho, put the rice noodles in a large bowl and pour boiling water over them. Let them sit for about 15 minutes to soften, then drain.

Heat the soup to piping hot. Prepare a large platter of the garnishes: a big pile of mint, cilantro, and basil sprigs, slivered scallions and chiles, and lime wedges.

Line up the soup bowls (I love the deep, giant Chinatown-style bowls). Put a handful of noodles in each soup bowl and scatter some bean sprouts on top. Add a few raw onion slices. Ladle the broth and a bit of boiled meat into each bowl. Pass the platter of garnishes and let everyone add herbs, scallions, and chiles and a squeeze of lime.

Black Sticky Rice Pudding with Coconut Cream

Even though there are rice noodles in the pho, this extraordinarily yummy rice pudding (which I first encountered in Thailand) makes sense to me as a dessert to follow pho. This pudding is made with nutty, unpolished purply-black sticky rice.

Note: Thai sticky rice (often labeled sweet rice or glutinous rice) must be soaked before cooking.

1½ cups white sticky rice
1½ cups black sticky rice
2 cups coconut milk, fresh or canned

½ cup packed brown sugar or crushed palm sugar
1 teaspoon salt

Put the rice in a bowl, cover with cold water, and soak at least 4 hours or overnight. Drain.

Steam the rice in the traditional way, which is in a basket, fine-meshed strainer, or colander lined with cheesecloth set over boiling water. (It's possible to do it in an electric rice cooker, but the texture suffers.) Steam both rices together over rapidly boiling water for about 20 minutes, loosely covered with a lid, until the rice forms a solid mass. Carefully flip the rice over, cover the steamer, and steam it for another 20 minutes. When the rice is cooked, spread it out in a low bowl or on a platter and let cool for about 15 minutes.

Heat the coconut milk in a small saucepan with the sugar and salt, stirring to dissolve the sugar. Pour the coconut milk mixture over the rice and gently mix; it'll be a bit on the soupy side. Spoon it into a serving bowl, cover, and keep at cool room temperature for up to a few hours.

To serve, spoon the pudding into tiny bowls or onto pieces of banana leaf—a beautiful way to eat it. The idea is to have just a small portion to eat with a spoon.

Summer Menus

menu six
SPICES FOR A SUMMER NIGHT
Tabbouleh

Pita with Za'atar and Olive Oil

Tomatoes and Olives with Coriander Vinaigrette

Spicy Lamb Burgers with Grilled Eggplant

Cucumbers and Yogurt

Apricot Tart

menu seven
DINNER ON THE ITALIAN SIDE
Zucchini Antipasto with Fresh Mozzarella

Spaghetti with Squid and White Beans

Frozen Cappuccino

Digestivo with Fresh Berries

menu eight
THE PROMISE OF OLD BREAD
Halibut Crudo with Lemon Oil

Layered Tomato and Bread Salad

Fresh Peach Ice Cream

menu nine
HOW TO FRY FISH
Stand-Around Melon with Mint

Fish Fry with Piquant Tarragon Mayonnaise

Green Bean Salad with Pickled Shallots

Salt-Roasted New Potatoes

Lemon Pound Cake with Peaches and Berries

menu ten
PARSLEY GOES WITH EVERYTHING
Chilled Tomato Soup with Basil

Flat-Roasted Chicken with Rosemary

Rice Salad with Sweet Herbs

Lemon Verbena Bavarian Cream

Spices for a Summer Night

Tabbouleh
Pita with Za'atar and Olive Oil
Tomatoes and Olives with Coriander Vinaigrette
Spicy Lamb Burgers with Grilled Eggplant
Cucumbers and Yogurt
Apricot Tart

It's the longest day of the year, and the moon is full on Bob's farm in Sonoma. On a warm summer night like this, I somehow yearn for the seasonings of the Middle East. Maybe it's because we've spent the golden afternoon hours picking eggplants, tomatoes, chiles, and cilantro from his gardens. It's like shooting fish in a barrel—you can't help eating the vegetables raw in the field, and they really taste like something. We set the table just steps away from the outdoor kitchen, with sinks for washing vegetables. You can't get any more garden-to-table than that. Now we're getting hungry, and it becomes obvious that it's time to open the first bottle of something cold and pink.

Bob is an old Sonoma hippie, the consummate male version of an earth mother; he's lived on the land for thirty years or more and knows everything that matters about growing vegetables, companion planting, biodynamic farming, the mutual benefits of weeds and plants. His studied yet scruffy approach involves cutting back the weeds, then eventually letting them grow up around the plants until everything is just wild. It's a way of gardening that imitates nature. He doesn't try to restrain plants, he nurtures their livelihood. Bob takes the long view.

There are herb beds everywhere, total hedges of lemon verbena, and thyme of every variety, and we pound together a little mixture to spread on the bread we're about to grill. We set out the whole meal on Bob's long picnic table. As we assemble our platters, all those beautiful dishes—made more lovely by their proximity and variety—look to me like hospitality itself. When we sit down, we're down for the duration. No running back and forth to the kitchen. It is an idyllic Sonoma night, hot, but with an ocean breeze coming over the mountains. We feel far away from the world, even though we're only half an hour from the highway.

Tabbouleh

A properly made tabbouleh is really a parsley salad with a little bulgur wheat, not the other way around, as most Americans know it.

¾ cup bulgur wheat

Salt and pepper

Juice of 2 lemons, or to taste

4 scallions, finely minced

½ cup mint leaves, finely chopped

¼ cup olive oil, or to taste

3 cups parsley leaves,
   coarsely chopped

1 pint cherry tomatoes, halved

Soak the bulgur in cold water for 30 minutes.

Dump the grains in a colander and give it a good shake to drain. Put a clean dish towel in a salad bowl and gather up the drained bulgur to further dry it. Gently remove the towel, put the bulgur in a bowl, and begin to assemble the tabbouleh: Season the grains generously with salt and pepper, then stir in the lemon juice and toss well. Add the scallions and mint and toss. Drizzle in 3 tablespoons of the oil, and then taste and adjust the seasoning. Add half the parsley and mix well.

Spoon the tabbouleh onto a platter, and sprinkle the rest of the parsley over the top. Put the cherry tomatoes in a little bowl, season them with salt and pepper and the remaining tablespoon of olive oil, and spoon them over the top of the salad.

ZA'ATAR

I learned about za'atar from my sister, who encountered it, oddly enough, in Switzerland when she lived there. This sister, a nice Jewish girl, told me she learned about za'atar from an expat Palestinian woman who taught her to eat it with bread and olive oil. It became a symbol of their friendship.

Za'atar is an herb mixture known throughout the Middle East. Its base is a kind of wild oregano (aka Bible hyssop or *Origanum syriacum*), which is said to be the original za'atar herb. Every country has its own version, and the mix usually contains (in various proportions) wild thyme, sumac, and sesame seed. There's a wide variety of za'atars available by mail or in Middle Eastern shops: Syrian, Israeli, Jordanian, and Lebanese. Some are heavy on powdered sumac, made from sour red sumac berries; others use only a little sumac and are greener.

I eat za'atar as my sister showed me—on pita bread dipped in olive oil—but it tastes good on many other things too. I like it on yogurt or labneh (yogurt cheese), or over slices of utterly fresh mozzarella. It's also delicious sprinkled on fried eggs or roast chicken.

Pita with Za'atar and Olive Oil

It's always fun going through a Middle Eastern grocery, chockablock with all manner of spices, grains, beans, baklava, and Turkish coffeepots. There's such a market in almost every big North American city. Most carry a wide assortment of breads, like good-quality pita and flat slabs of freshly baked lavash. In a pinch, use a loaf of fresh French bread.

Check out the spice bins in the market for za'atar. For a homemade version, you can use this blend.

FOR THE ZA'ATAR

¼ cup fresh marjoram leaves

2 tablespoons sesame seeds

¼ cup dried thyme

2 tablespoons dried oregano

2 tablespoons powdered sumac
  (optional)

2 teaspoons coarse sea salt

Pita bread

Olive oil

Heat a small dry cast-iron skillet over medium-high heat. Add the marjoram leaves and let them toast and dry a bit, stirring with a wooden spoon, about 2 minutes. Remove them to a bowl. Add the sesame seeds to the hot pan, stirring them as they toast a bit. Add to the bowl with the marjoram, along with the thyme, oregano, sumac (if using), and coarse salt. Transfer to an electric spice grinder or a mortar and grind or pound them to a rough powder. Put the za'atar in a small dish.

Warm the bread and cut into quarters. Pour some good fruity olive oil into a shallow bowl. Dip the bread in the oil, then sprinkle it with a pinch of za'atar.

Tomatoes and Olives with Coriander Vinaigrette

You can prepare the vinaigrette in advance, minus the cilantro, then dress this salad at the last minute. I like the combination of toasted coriander and sweet ripe tomatoes.

¼ cup finely diced red onion

1 garlic clove, smashed to a paste with a little salt

2 tablespoons red wine vinegar

Salt and pepper

½ cup olive oil

1 teaspoon coriander seeds

Pinch of cayenne

2 pounds ripe tomatoes, various sizes and colors

½ cup good green olives, such as picholine, not pitted

½ cup oil-cured black olives, not pitted

1 cup cilantro leaves, roughly chopped

In a small bowl, mix the vinaigrette, starting with the onion, garlic, vinegar, and salt and pepper. Stir in the olive oil.

Toast the coriander seeds in a dry skillet over medium-high heat until fragrant. Transfer to an electric spice grinder or a mortar and grind or pound to a powder. Stir into the vinaigrette and add the cayenne.

Cut the tomatoes into thick slices and arrange in a random pattern on a large serving platter. Season lightly with salt. Scatter the green and black olives over the top.

Just before serving, check the vinaigrette's seasoning, and stir in the chopped cilantro. Spoon the vinaigrette over the tomatoes.

Spicy Lamb Burgers with Grilled Eggplant

These pan-Mediterranean lamb burgers are spicy and fragrant. If you have a nice butcher, get him to grind the lamb for you. I like to use ground shoulder for these burgers. MAKES 24 SKEWERS OR LITTLE BURGERS

FOR THE BURGERS

3 pounds ground lamb shoulder

1 small onion, grated

½ cup chopped parsley

2 tablespoons finely chopped mint

2 teaspoons finely chopped marjoram

6 garlic cloves, smashed to a paste with a little salt

2 teaspoons cumin seeds, toasted and ground

2 teaspoons coriander seeds, toasted and ground

1 teaspoon ground cinnamon

2 teaspoons salt

1 teaspoon pepper

½ teaspoon cayenne

½ teaspoon red pepper flakes

3 large eggplants, sliced into ½-inch-thick circles

2 tablespoons olive oil

Salt and pepper

To make the burgers, mix the lamb and all the remaining ingredients together well. Chill for several hours. (You can season the lamb a day ahead and refrigerate overnight.)

When you're ready to serve, prepare a fire in a charcoal grill. Paint the eggplant slices with the olive oil and season on both sides with salt and pepper. Grill the slices over hot coals for about 2 minutes per side. Remove to a large serving platter.

Divide the seasoned meat into 24 portions. Form each into a sausage shape about 4 inches long, and insert a slender skewer into each one. Or form patties and cook them like burgers. Grill over hot coals, turning once, about 3 minutes per side, so the lamb stays juicy.

Put the lamb burgers over the eggplant slices on the platter and serve.

Cucumbers and Yogurt

You can think of this as a salad or as a saucy accompaniment to everything else on the menu. I like it on the more yogurty side, but you could add twice as much cucumber.

1 large cucumber, peeled, sliced,
   and cut into half moons
Salt and pepper
2 cups whole-milk yogurt
1 garlic clove, smashed to a paste
   with a little salt

2 tablespoons olive oil
1 tablespoon chopped mint
1 tablespoon chopped dill
1 tablespoon chopped chives
Red pepper flakes or slivered
   fresh hot chile

Put the cucumber in a bowl and season with salt and pepper. Add the yogurt, garlic, olive oil, mint, dill, and chives and stir it all together. Spoon into a serving bowl and chill for at least an hour.

Just before serving, sprinkle with red pepper flakes or slivers of fresh hot chile.

Apricot Tart

Apricots have a very short season, and you've got to make the most of them when they're around. Stone fruit is prone to the vagaries of the weather, so if there's a frost when the trees are blooming, there will be no fruit that year—which makes apricots even more precious. This simple little farmhouse tart celebrates apricots at their peak of ripeness. It's a little bit counterintuitive, but even ripe apricots need abundant sugar to bring out their sweetness. Otherwise, the tart will be too tart.

1 cup all-purpose flour, plus more for sprinkling

About ½ cup sugar, plus more for sprinkling

Pinch of salt

8 tablespoons (1 stick) cold butter, cut into very small pieces

¼ cup ice water

1 pound firm but ripe apricots

¼ cup water

Put the flour, ½ teaspoon of the sugar, and the salt into a mixing bowl, and work in 4 tablespoons of the butter with your fingers until it is well incorporated. Add the remaining butter, leaving it in little chunks. Stir in the ice water.

Gather the dough into a ball, wrap in plastic wrap, and then squash it into a disk. Refrigerate for at least an hour.

On a lightly floured surface, roll out the dough into a circle approximately 14 inches in diameter. Transfer to a large baking sheet lined with parchment and refrigerate while you prepare the apricots and make the glaze.

With a sharp paring knife, cut the apricots in half to remove the pits, then cut into quarters. Roughly chop ½ cup of the apricots for the glaze. In a small saucepan, bring the chopped apricots, ½ cup sugar, and the ¼ cup water to a brisk simmer and cook for about 20 minutes; strain and cool.

Preheat the oven to 375°F. Sprinkle the circle of dough with about a tablespoon of flour, to keep it from getting soggy. Leaving a 2-inch border, arrange the apricot quarters skin side down in concentric circles until you've covered the entire surface of the pastry. Trim an inch from the edge of the pastry and gently fold up the remaining edge over the fruit. Sprinkle the fruit and the overlapping pastry generously with sugar.

Bake the tart for 35 to 40 minutes, until the pastry is nicely browned and the edges of the apricots are slightly caramelized.

Carefully slide the tart, still on its parchment, onto a cooling rack. While the tart is still warm, paint the apricots with the glaze. Serve at room temperature.

Dinner on the Italian Side

Zucchini Antipasto with Fresh Mozzarella
Spaghetti with Squid and White Beans
Frozen Cappuccino
Digestivo with Fresh Berries

I've spent years in France, and although I truly love being there, it's always a surprising thrill to cross the border into Italy. Take a walk down the main *strada* in anytown Italy—it feels so wonderfully *Italian*. Even the most unprepossessing little food shops have bright crostini in their windows, and the bars and *caffès* and markets are always lively. And the espresso is the best in the world. I love how in summer the restaurants close their dining rooms and seat everyone outside. The food is easier—gutsy and restrained at the same time. And then there's pasta, which the French don't really understand.

In a small Tuscan town, lunch at Tony's sort-of Uncle Luciano's evokes a reverie on pasta. When pasta is cooked correctly and tossed with just enough sauce to make it flavorful, you honor the pasta. It's not swimming in sauce like those big-bowl main courses many Americans love. The pasta course in a formal Italian meal is just a small taste of pasta. Or there are spaghetti feasts, where people sit outside at long tables and properly

prepared platters of pasta are passed along, like a scene from an old Italian movie. Humble pasta becomes the centerpiece of these gatherings.

Luciano himself is a bit scruffy, with a big head of white hair and a beard. He usually wears a cap, and though he's not fat, he obviously appreciates a good meal. He loves to take you around town and get you the best coffee here, the best grappa there. He'll step into any bar and strike up a conversation. He invites us home to lunch, in a house his girlfriend, Tony's Aunt Maria (they're both in their late seventies), refuses to enter. She says his house is too dirty. He has courted the elusive Maria for the last twenty or thirty years, leaving her jewelry on her windowsill, but she won't give him the time of day, except to invite him to dinner occasionally. His kitchen is so bachelor-cluttery, it looks as if it hasn't been cleaned in years. Maria has a point.

Uncle Luciano loves to cook, and he likes to think of himself as a gourmet. He's especially passionate about pasta. "If you have pasta and anchovy and some garlic, you will never starve!" he tells us. "You can always make yourself a meal." The pasta he serves us is an intensely flavored version of *spaghetti aglio, olio, e peperoncino*—garlic, olive oil, and hot red pepper. With the water boiling and the spaghetti in, he pours some olive oil into the skillet on the stove and tosses in a good handful of chopped garlic, smashed fennel seeds, wild oregano, and hot red pepper flakes. Only at the end does he stir in anchovies from a tin, rinsed and chopped, and let them melt into the oil. Drain the pasta, put it in a bowl, and toss it with the delicious oil. That's the recipe! But make sure the pasta is perfectly al dente.

Zucchini Antipasto with Fresh Mozzarella

You know those little trattorie, where you're greeted by a table full of dozens of dishes of antipasti, mostly simple vegetables, like *cippoline in agro-dolce* (sweet-and-sour onions), marinated mushrooms, and grilled eggplant? This zucchini is just one of the platters on that table. You could add other vegetables, but there's something wonderful about just zucchini.

2 pounds medium zucchini
Salt and pepper
Olive oil
A few basil leaves and mint leaves

1 tablespoon chopped chives
Half a lemon
Sliced fresh mozzarella
(optional)

Preheat the broiler. Cut the zucchini into ½-inch-thick slices, either long or round. Season the slices on both sides with salt and pepper. Put the slices on a baking sheet and drizzle with olive oil. Broil them until they color lightly on the first side. Flip the slices and broil the other side. (Of course, you can do the zucchini on a charcoal grill or even in a cast-iron skillet.)

Arrange the zucchini on a platter, overlapping the slices. You can do this up to 2 hours ahead.

Just before serving, roughly chop the basil and mint leaves, and scatter them, with the chopped chives, over the zucchini. Squeeze the lemon over the platter, and give it another drizzle of olive oil. Serve with slices of fresh mozzarella, if you like.

A SQUID LESSON

When you look for squid in a fish store, you want to see it just glistening, the eyes clear and gorgeous. Most fish stores that sell cleaned squid are selling frozen squid. It's obviously better to buy fresh squid and clean it yourself. It's so unbelievably easy to do, it takes about ten seconds per squid.

At the restaurant, we clean about twenty-five pounds at a time, but I find it a completely enjoyable task. An old Chinese guy who was in charge of cutting fish in one of the first restaurants I cooked at in San Francisco taught me how. It's worth learning his very efficient method. The key is never putting down the knife (it stays firmly in one hand) and using your free hand to maneuver the squid.

Here's the method: Lay the squid on a cutting board, tentacles stage right. With a sharp knife, cut off the tentacles just above the eyes, then gently touch the tentacles with the side of the knife and pop out the little round "beak." Pluck away the beak with the left hand. With the knife blade, grab the tip of the cellophane-like quill at the top of the body, and, holding the quill with the knife, tug the squid body backward with the left hand. Then press the back of the knife against the body to squeeze out the innards. It takes more time to describe than to do it.

Spaghetti with Squid and White Beans

This is essentially *spaghetti aglio, olio, e peperoncino,* with more clothes on. If you can't find good fresh squid, make the dish with shrimp or grilled rare tuna. Basil or rosemary is a fine substitute for the marjoram. To make it vegetarian, skip the squid and add chopped fresh tomato. In the time it takes to boil the pasta, the sauce will be ready.

1 pound spaghetti or bucatini

2 pounds squid, cleaned, bodies sliced into 1-inch rings, tentacles chopped

½ cup olive oil, plus extra for drizzling

Salt and pepper

3 large garlic cloves, smashed to a paste with a little salt

1 teaspoon red pepper flakes

1 tablespoon chopped marjoram

2 cups cooked white beans, warmed

Bring a large pot of salted water to a boil. Add the pasta and cook until al dente.

Meanwhile, put the squid in a colander, rinse briefly, and pat dry. Heat the olive oil in a large deep skillet over high heat. Make sure the oil is good and hot. Carefully add the squid; the oil will splatter at first. Season generously with salt and pepper and stir with a wooden spoon. Quickly add the garlic, pepper flakes, and marjoram and cook for no more than a minute. Then stir in the white beans.

When the pasta is al dente, drain and add it to the skillet. Add salt and a drizzle of olive oil, toss quickly, and transfer to a serving bowl.

{VARIATION} SALAD OF SQUID AND WHITE BEANS
For an easy first course, omit the pasta. Pile the warm squid and beans onto a platter, surround with slices of tomato and sweet onion, and drizzle with olive oil.

CRAZY FOR SQUID

In America, we only know pretty much one size of squid, but they have an enormous range—from as tiny as your fingernail to bigger than a speedboat. The pervasive and insipid fried calamari, which has somehow become our standard bar food, is worlds away from expertly fried squid. When I'm in Italy, I'm crazy about the little fried *calamaretti*. I love the *chipirones,* baby squid, in Spain. There's a little place in Seville where you can buy them hot from the fryer served in a paper cone. Something about those crisp, teeny tiny squid that you eat whole completely gets me.

At home, oven-roasted squid is easy and wonderful. Start with small squid, say about 4 inches or less, cleaned and tentacles and bodies separated. Season them with olive oil, salt, and pepper, put both the tentacles and bodies on a baking sheet, and throw them in a hot oven (450°F) for about 15 minutes, until they're puffed up a bit and browned. Sprinkle with garlic and parsley.

In Asia, life without squid—in soups and stir-fries—would be unthinkable. Squid marries so well with ginger, garlic, and cilantro. I like to think of it as the pork of the sea, and, in fact, squid is very good with pork—with Chinese sausage, for instance. Dried squid is really popular in Southeast Asia but virtually unknown outside of Asian cuisine. A common street food in Thailand is whole dried squid toasted over coals, then run through the pins of a hand-cranked roller. It comes out thin as paper, and you eat it almost like chips, dipped in a spicy sauce.

And let's not forget the wonderful things you can do with cuttlefish ink, which is richer and darker than squid ink. Cuttlefish is a firm-fleshed cousin of the squid, equally delicious. I always find it fascinating that in Italy cuttlefish in its own ink alongside a slice of polenta is considered everyday fare, just as a slice of meat loaf would be in Philadelphia. When you make the black sauce, with undertones of tomato and garlic and saffron, the ink imparts a flavor as deep as the ocean, with a surprising sweetness. Added to a dish like *spaghetti nero* or risotto, it has the intensity of wine.

Frozen Cappuccino

This frozen dessert for a very hot day begins with the best Italian roasted espresso beans. Make the strongest espresso you can in a stovetop or other espresso maker—or go to your corner coffee bar and get espresso to go; it doesn't have to be hot. Use the best cream you can find—it does make a difference.

2 cups espresso coffee
½ cup plus 1 to 2 tablespoons
   sugar, or to taste

1 cup organic heavy cream

Stir the coffee and ½ cup of the sugar together to dissolve the sugar, and pour the mixture into a Pyrex baking dish or other flat pan. Taste for sweetness. It should be rather sweet; add more sugar if necessary. Cover and put in the freezer overnight.

The next day, pull the pan from the freezer and let it thaw a bit. When it's just a bit mushy, chop it roughly with a metal spatula. Then return the pan to the freezer until ready to serve.

Whip the cream with the remaining 1 to 2 tablespoons sugar until barely thickened.

To serve, spoon the granita into short glasses or espresso cups, and top generously with whipped cream. (For extra-caffeinated decadence, pour another shot of hot or cold espresso over the top.) Serve with biscotti.

Digestivo with Fresh Berries

In Italian Alpine towns, many restaurants will bring you a complimentary shot of grappa with berries along with the check. This charming gesture softens the blow.

1 cup fresh berries (a mixture of   2 tablespoons sugar
    raspberries and blackberries)   2 cups grappa or vodka

Put the berries in a bowl, sprinkle with the sugar, and crush the berries with your hands. Add the grappa or vodka, cover, and refrigerate for at least a few hours. (The mixture will keep for about 2 months in the refrigerator.)

Serve in small glasses, using a ladle to make sure every glass has some berries.

The Promise of Old Bread

Halibut Crudo with Lemon Oil
Layered Tomato and Bread Salad
Fresh Peach Ice Cream

Sheep, it turns out, adore bread. When I worked as a cook in a château in the Dordogne, we saved all our old baguettes for the château's herd of sheep, who'd look forward to our daily visits. Until you have seen a French ewe come running at the sight of the day-old-bread truck, you have not seen everything. The baguettes also served to distract the sheep if you needed to grab one by the hind legs for a feast of spit-roasted whole lamb, the grand *mechoui.* But that is another story.

Bread has always been revered in Europe as a kind of birthright, and a treasure never to be wasted. Before home ovens were commonplace, you'd take your roasts and casseroles to the community oven to cook on the hot wood-fired stone. When the heat dropped to the right temperature you'd make a few pizzas or fruit tarts. Afterward you would bake your bread.

Because fresh bread was only a once-a-week phenomenon in many homes, techniques were developed for dealing with stale bread. Though toasting always improves day-old bread, another way to keep good country bread chewable and tasty over time is to slice it ever thinner each day, until at last it is no thicker than a wafer.

Ingenious slotted cutting boards were devised to catch the crumbs that were a by-product of the process of slicing bread, and the crumbs were carefully saved to use later. Inevitably, though, there were bits of hard bread left over. These, too, were saved, and there were many uses for them.

A slice of dry bread in a bowl of soup was commonplace. Old bread, rubbed with garlic, became croutons for salad; old bread soaked in milk made a fish cake go further. Little toasts were saved for the aperitif. Crusts moistened with tomato, oil, and vinegar became a salad. Spanish-style *migas*—rough cubes of bread fried in olive oil—also proved a tasty resurrection.

I find this reverence for bread entirely praiseworthy. It shows respect for the farmer, the miller, and the baker. But more than that, the dishes derived from old bread can be downright delicious.

Halibut Crudo with Lemon Oil

It doesn't get much simpler than this. Crudo is basically Italian-style sashimi. You slice good fresh fish sashimi-thin (about ⅛ inch thick), and lay the fish on a platter. Everything should be quite cold. You can slice the fish an hour ahead and keep it chilled, then drizzle with the herbed lemon oil just before serving.

1 pound fillets halibut or other
   sushi-quality fish
Salt and pepper
Grated zest and juice of ½ lemon

1 tablespoon olive oil
1 tablespoon thinly sliced chives
   or slivered scallions

Slice the fish across the grain into 16 thin slices. Arrange on a chilled platter. Season each slice with salt and pepper.

Whisk together the lemon zest and juice, olive oil, and chives or scallions. Spoon over the fish and serve.

Layered Tomato and Bread Salad

This bread salad can be the main course of a light lunch or a simple summer supper. Some versions call for soaking the bread in water first and squeezing it out, but that's not what I'm after here. What I like about this salad is that some of the bread stays crisp and some softens. SERVES 4 TO 6

12 slices day-old country bread, such as pain au levain

½ cup olive oil, plus more for brushing

3 garlic cloves, smashed to a paste with a little salt, plus a few garlic cloves for swiping the bread

1 shallot, minced

3 tablespoons red wine vinegar

6 anchovy fillets, coarsely chopped

1 tablespoon capers, rinsed and roughly chopped

½ cup niçoise olives, pitted and roughly chopped

Salt and pepper

6 ripe large tomatoes, roughly cubed

1 small cucumber, peeled and sliced

A generous handful of basil leaves, roughly chopped

A generous handful of parsley leaves, roughly chopped

Lettuce leaves

Preheat the oven to 400°F. Paint the bread generously with olive oil on both sides and place it on a baking sheet. Bake until the slices are crisp and golden, about 10 minutes, turning them halfway through. (Or toast the oil-painted bread on a grill.) Let the bread cool, and swipe each slice with a garlic clove. Break each slice into 2 or 3 pieces. Set aside.

To make the vinaigrette, macerate the shallot in the vinegar for 5 minutes. Stir in the garlic paste and add the ½ cup olive oil. Add the anchovies, capers, and olives and stir well. Season to taste with salt and pepper.

Put the tomato cubes and cucumber slices in a medium bowl and season well with salt and pepper. Pour the vinaigrette over the vegetables.

Assemble the salad on a deep platter or in a low wide bowl: Layer half the bread slices on the platter or in the bowl and spoon over half of the tomato/cucumber mixture. Lay over the rest of the bread and top with the remaining tomatoes. Cover with a clean towel and let sit for about an hour at cool room temperature.

Just before serving, gently press down the salad with your hands to distribute the juices. Sprinkle generously with the basil and parsley. Spoon the salad onto plates lined with crisp lettuce leaves.

MAKING BREAD CRUMBS

Homemade bread crumbs have a certain kind of charm. They're not all the same size, and their texture is real and rough; they're just more "crumby." Old, powdery, tasteless store-bought bread crumbs don't come close to being in the same league.

There are crumbs, crumbs, and crumbs. With good dry bread, you can have coarse, rough-torn bits, or you can have fine ones if you wish. You may have to put the bread in a low oven to dry or leave it out overnight. A good way to make them is to put them in a large bowl and crush them with the bottom of a wine bottle. Some prefer the kitchen-towel-and-rolling-pin method. (For that matter, the one thing a food processor really does well is to make bread crumbs.) Coarse dry bread crumbs are ideal for sizzling. Crisp them in a pan with a little butter or olive oil and freshly ground black pepper. These crunchy, warm, peppery crumbs are delicious sprinkled on a steaming bowl of garlicky spaghetti. Of course, they're good on vegetables, too, or for topping gratins and baked casseroles.

With a day-old or two-day-old white French loaf or baguette—one that's made with unbleached flour, water, and salt—you can make soft, moist "fresh" crumbs. These are great for breading, for instance, a piece of fish, or for fried oysters. Remove the crust with a serrated knife and cut the bread into 1-inch cubes. Put them in the food processor and pulse until you have relatively uniform, fluffy crumbs. Dip your fish (or chicken breast) into seasoned flour, then beaten egg. Coat lightly with the crumbs and shallow-fry gently until golden. The texture of this breading is both crisp and tender.

Fresh Peach Ice Cream

There's something absolutely summery about freshly churned peach ice cream. You do need to make the custard ahead to give it time to cool.

1½ cups heavy cream
½ cup sugar, plus more for
   sugaring the peaches
4 egg yolks

¼ teaspoon vanilla extract
1 pound ripe sweet peaches
2 tablespoons honey

Put the cream and sugar in a saucepan over medium heat and bring to just under a simmer, stirring to dissolve the sugar.

Beat the egg yolks with the vanilla in a separate bowl. Stir in a little of the warm cream just to warm up the yolks, then pour the mixture back into the pan. Turn the heat to low and cook, stirring constantly and making sure it does not boil, for about 5 minutes. Strain the mixture into a bowl and chill until cool.

Peel and pit the peaches. Coarsely chop them and put them in a bowl. Sprinkle with about 2 tablespoons sugar, add the honey, and then squeeze the peach chunks with your hands to mash them roughly.

Pour the custard into your ice cream freezer and churn it until the custard is quite thick. Only then add the peaches, so that you keep the integrity of the fruit, and finish churning the ice cream.

How to Fry Fish

Stand-Around Melon with Mint
Fish Fry with Piquant Tarragon Mayonnaise
Green Bean Salad with Pickled Shallots
Salt-Roasted New Potatoes
Lemon Pound Cake with Peaches and Berries

I tried out for a job once on Fisherman's Wharf in San Francisco. At the time, I was about twenty-one, a young cook looking for a gig. There was a headhunter named Maxine, and she was a piece of work. She had a certain Katharine Hepburn-y kind of style. Instead of a pompadour, she wore her silver hair in a pageboy. Every day, in a crisp skirt, heels, scarf, and jewelry, with perfect nails, she'd go for lunch at the World Trade Center in the Ferry Plaza. She was kind of WWII-era San Francisco, but getting on in years, with that same shoulder-padded, slim-but-tough look as my high school English teacher.

Maxine had a wood-paneled office, and cooks would come from all over San Francisco. While you sat on her sofa, Maxine would flip through her Rolodex and pick up the phone: "Chef? I have a young cook here and he has no experience, but he's good!" Then she'd look over her reading glasses and say, "I have a job for you."

Maxine sent me off to one of those well-known fish houses on Fisherman's Wharf. I think it was Scoma's. Most of the kitchen was Filipino cooks, plus a few hard-core Anglo former Marines, and a bevy of male Hungarian waiters in red jackets. There were no written orders. Everything was called out, and you had to remember each order. As soon as you heard it, you'd put it in. On my first night, my job was to do the Captain's Platter, which consisted of six fried shrimp, six fried scallops, six oysters, and six chunks of cod. You had your deep-fat fryer with one basket for each ingredient.

Well, as it turned out, the Captain's Platter was a really popular item. Not only did you have to get the pieces of seafood fried, you had to get them out of the fryer and into the napkins that were folded just so, with a pocket for each type. It quickly became all too clear that I was neither fast enough nor athletic enough for the Captain's Platter. The chef, an older Filipino man, had to step in and help me out. At the end of the evening, he gave me a gentle smile as he handed me a check for one day's wages.

The next day I went back to see Maxine.

Stand-Around Melon with Mint

When you're frying fish, you can't have a sit-down first course. So you get to stand around and eat this delicious melon while you're waiting for the fish to fry.

1 small cantaloupe   1 or 2 limes, halved
1 small honeydew melon   A handful of mint leaves

If you're making melon balls, just cut the melons in half, remove the seeds, and, using a melon baller, proceed to make as many melon balls as you can from each half. Otherwise, peel the melons as follows: Cut each melon in half and cut each half into 4 pieces. Slide your knife between the flesh and the peel, then cut the peel-less wedges into uniform bite-size pieces. Put the melon in a bowl and refrigerate until cold.

Just before serving, squeeze lime juice over the melon. Cut the mint leaves into slivers; scatter over the melons, toss lightly, and pile onto a platter. Pass the toothpicks.

Fish Fry with Piquant Tarragon Mayonnaise

Fried foods have a bad rep in two ways: people are convinced anything fried is really bad for you, and they think frying is an impossible chore. Neither has to be the case. Of course, a steady diet of all things fried is not good for anybody, but done well and with a delicate hand, fried food is a delight.

I'm not talking about investing in a deep-fat fryer, I'm talking about shallow-fried fish, which is completely doable when you have a couple of cast-iron pans going on the stovetop at the same time.

It's not so much a matter of the batter, it's more about ensuring that the oil is at the right temperature and nursing the fish in the oil without touching it too much. Everyone has his own idea about what to coat the fish in, but the one I have come to like the most is a buttermilk and flour batter. The type of oil is another variable. It should be the least-processed, best vegetable oil you can find. I generally use sunflower or safflower oil.

Eight to ten 3-ounce pieces
   haddock, halibut, monkfish, or
   other firm white fish fillets
Salt and pepper
2 cups cultured buttermilk
Oil for frying

2 cups all-purpose flour
½ teaspoon cayenne
Parsley and/or watercress sprigs
Lemon wedges
Piquant Tarragon Mayonnaise
   (recipe follows)

Season each piece of fish with salt and pepper, and put in a shallow bowl. Pour the buttermilk over the fish and refrigerate for up to 2 hours, until you're ready to fry them.

Fill two cast-iron skillets about halfway with oil. Heat it to a temperature of 375°F on a deep-fat thermometer. When you reach that temperature, adjust the flame as necessary to maintain it. Put the flour on a large plate set next to the stove, and mix in the cayenne and a teaspoon each of salt and pepper.

{CONTINUED}

Remove the fish from the refrigerator and drain in a colander. One piece at a time, lightly coat the fish in the seasoned flour, then slip it gently into the oil, continuing until you have all the fish frying in the pans. Cook for about 3 minutes per side, turning gently. The fish will have a nice, puffy, golden brown exterior.

With a slotted spoon or spatula, carefully lift the fish from the oil and onto paper towels to drain, then transfer to a large platter. Surround the fish with parsley or watercress sprigs and lemon wedges, and get it to the table fast. Pass around the tarragon mayonnaise.

Piquant Tarragon Mayonnaise

It's well worth it to make homemade mayonnaise. It's worlds away from the store-bought kind, especially for this crispy fried fish.

2 egg yolks	Generous pinch of cayenne
1½ cups olive oil	Salt and pepper
Grated zest and juice of	1 teaspoon chopped tarragon
½ lemon, or to taste	1 teaspoon chopped chives
Dijon mustard	

Whisk the egg yolks in a bowl. Slowly whisk in 1 cup of the olive oil, a spoonful at a time at first, until an emulsion forms. Once the sauce thickens, you can continue whisking and add the oil in a slow, thin stream. When the mayonnaise is quite thick, add a little lemon zest and a good squeeze of lemon juice, a teaspoon or so of Dijon mustard, and the cayenne. Season with salt and pepper. Whisk in the remaining ½ cup olive oil. Thin the mayonnaise with a little water if necessary. Taste for seasoning, then stir in the chopped tarragon and chives.

The mayonnaise can be kept, refrigerated, for up to 2 days.

Green Bean Salad with Pickled Shallots

The beans can be cooked and the vinaigrette prepared ahead of time, then tossed together at the last minute.

3 large shallots

Salt and pepper

3 tablespoons sherry vinegar

2 pounds small green beans,
  topped and tailed

¼ cup olive oil

1 tablespoon finely slivered chives

Peel the shallots and slice crosswise. Put them in a small bowl, season well with salt and pepper, and add the vinegar. Let sit for a half hour.

Boil the green beans in a large pot of salted water for 3 to 5 minutes, until just past crunchy. Spread them out to cool. Just before you serve the salad, put the green beans in a bowl and season well with salt and pepper. Whisk the olive oil into the shallots and vinegar, then add the dressed shallots to the beans. Toss well, transfer to a platter or serving bowl, and sprinkle with the chives.

Salt-Roasted New Potatoes

Summer is the season for tiny new potatoes that you find at the farmers' market, like German Butterball, Russian Banana, and little fingerlings. Simply scrub them, add a little oil and salt, and roast them in the oven. Easy! Roasted potatoes are delicious with fried fish.

2 pounds tiny new potatoes

A few sprigs of thyme

1 small head garlic, broken into
  cloves, not peeled

Olive oil

Salt and pepper

Preheat the oven to 400°F. Wash the potatoes and pat them dry. Put them in a baking dish in one layer, and add the thyme and garlic cloves. Drizzle generously with olive oil and toss to coat everything well. Sprinkle with salt and pepper.

Cover the dish with foil and bake for about 30 minutes. When the potatoes are tender when tested with a fork, remove the foil and let them brown for another 10 to 15 minutes. Serve from their baking dish, with the roasted garlic, or pile on a platter.

Lemon Pound Cake with Peaches and Berries

A thin slice of pound cake with sugared peaches and berries is a perfect finish to this menu. The addition of cornmeal gives the cake excellent texture. The cake can be made in the morning or even the day before.

FOR THE POUND CAKE

½ pound (2 sticks) butter, softened

1 cup sugar

Grated zest of 2 lemons

4 eggs

½ teaspoon salt

¼ teaspoon vanilla extract

1 cup cake flour

½ cup finely ground cornmeal (or corn flour)

FOR THE GLAZE

½ cup sugar

Juice of the 2 zested lemons

1 tablespoon grappa or rum

FOR THE FRUIT

4 peaches or nectarines

1 pint raspberries

1 pint blackberries

2 to 3 tablespoons sugar

Juice of ½ lemon

To make the cake, preheat the oven to 350°F. Generously butter a loaf pan and dust with flour. In a mixing bowl, beat the butter, sugar, and lemon zest well until the mixture looks creamy, about 2 minutes. (An electric mixer is helpful.)

Beat the eggs with the salt and vanilla and slowly add to the butter mixture to incorporate, then beat well for about a minute.

Sift the flour and the cornmeal together, and slowly add this mixture to the mixing bowl. Beat for another minute, until it's well incorporated and the batter looks fluffy.

With a rubber spatula, scrape the batter into the loaf pan, and put the cake in the oven. Check for doneness with a table knife after about an hour. When the knife comes out dry, the cake is done. Cool for a few minutes, then unmold the cake onto a rack, turn right side up, and let cool.

To make the glaze, mix the sugar and lemon juice in a small saucepan. Bring to a boil, stirring to dissolve the sugar, and boil for 2 minutes. Take it off the heat and stir in the grappa or rum. Pour the glaze over the cake.

Peel and slice the peaches and put them in a bowl. Pick over the berries and add them to the peaches. Sprinkle with the sugar. Add the lemon juice and toss gently, cover the bowl, and refrigerate for up to several hours.

Serve slices of pound cake with a spoonful of the fruit compote and its juices.

MENU TEN

Parsley Goes with Everything

Chilled Tomato Soup with Basil
Flat-Roasted Chicken with Rosemary
Rice Salad with Sweet Herbs
Lemon Verbena Bavarian Cream

Nothing says summer more than the sudden abundance
of fresh herbs. Fragrant culinary herbs come in two categories. One is sweet:
parsley, chervil, basil, cilantro, mint, hyssop, lovage, chives, tarragon, and
dill. The other is resinous, which tend to be hardier, stemmier, and more
pungent: rosemary, thyme, marjoram, oregano, savory, and sage. Generally
speaking, sweet herbs combine well with one another, in a salad, say, or in
a salsa verde. Resinous herbs, used together, can make a flavorful marinade
for meat. And parsley, well, parsley goes with everything.

The resinous herbs dry best, and it's fine to use them dried in the dead
of winter, but when used fresh they have more flavor. Sweet herbs are
always better fresh. There's no comparing a jar of the dried stuff with the
sweetness of bright fresh flat-leaf parsley or basil.

Though herb mixtures have their uses, there's something appealingly
deliberate about cooking with only one herb—basil pesto, for instance.
I knew a cook in New York who learned to make pesto from an Italian
chef. He picked all the basil leaves from their stalks, laid them on a clean

tablecloth in the dining room, and let them sit out overnight in the cool, dark restaurant. The next day he'd make up a big batch of pesto.

Chopping fresh herbs at the last moment—to prevent their flavorful essential oils from dissipating—really does make a difference. If you don't believe me, chop a little parsley in the morning and taste it in the afternoon.

Whenever I can, I keep a few pots of fresh herbs on my windowsill. Often you need only a couple of sprigs for a dish, and it's so gratifying just to cut off a sprig or two instead of running to the supermarket and paying something exorbitant for more than you need.

Chilled Tomato Soup with Basil

If you've got really ripe, juicy garden tomatoes, this is the simplest gazpacho possible. If you don't have sweet, meaty tomatoes, fuggedaboudit! Those imperfect field-ripened and cracked specimens work well in this soup. I can't remember who first showed me how to grate tomatoes on the large holes of a box grater, but besides being the fastest, best way to get a little tomato puree, it's the only way to achieve the right texture here.

8 to 10 large ripe tomatoes

Salt and pepper

2 garlic cloves, smashed to a paste with a little salt

3 tablespoons olive oil

Mixed basil leaves for garnish

Wash the tomatoes and cut them in half. Put the box grater in a big mixing bowl. Grate the tomato halves against the large holes, rubbing back and forth until only the tomato skin remains in your hand.

Pour the tomato pulp into a coarse-mesh strainer set over another mixing bowl. Push the pulp through the strainer with a wooden spoon, leaving the seeds behind. To this bowl of gorgeous ruby puree, add salt and pepper to taste, the garlic, and olive oil. Stir well. Pour into a serving bowl.

Chill the soup well for about an hour. Just before serving, garnish the soup with a scattering of basil leaves.

{VARIATION} TOMATO SOUP AND SALAD

For an easy lunch, ladle this soup into wide soup bowls and spoon in a salad of chopped cucumbers and cherry tomatoes, seasoned with garlic, basil, a drop or two of red wine vinegar, and a generous amount of good olive oil.

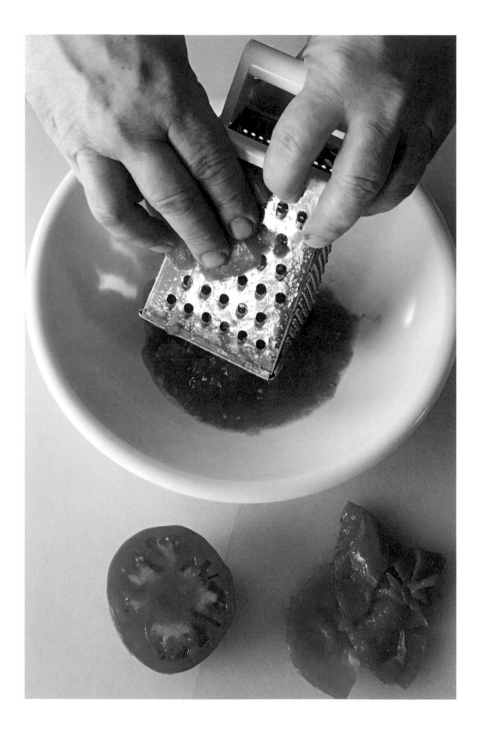

Flat-Roasted Chicken with Rosemary

This cooking method yields the most succulent bird, with lots of crisp, caramelized skin and the intense, satisfying flavor of garlic and rosemary. It's easy to do in a hot oven in a low roasting pan or a very large cast-iron pan. It goes without saying, the quality of the chicken matters above all.

This method also works well with game hens.

1 organic chicken, about 3 pounds	2 teaspoons red pepper flakes
Salt and pepper	Olive oil
¼ cup rosemary leaves	1 lemon, sliced
6 large garlic cloves, sliced	

Wash the bird and pat it dry. Remove the backbone with a pair of poultry shears or with a sharp knife. Push down on the breastbone to open the bird like a book.

Put the chicken in a roasting pan and season generously on both sides with salt and pepper. Sprinkle with the rosemary, garlic, and red pepper flakes. Drizzle with about 2 tablespoons of olive oil. Now, with your hands, gently smear the seasonings all over the bird.

Turn the chicken breast side up in the roasting pan, top with the lemon slices, cover, and refrigerate a couple of hours.

Bring the chicken to room temperature. Preheat the oven to 400°F. Roast the chicken for about an hour, or until it is beautifully browned and the juices run clear from the leg when pierced. Remove from the oven and let rest for 15 minutes.

Put the bird on a cutting board and cut into 6 portions with a heavy knife or a cleaver.

Rice Salad with Sweet Herbs

Like a good potato salad, a good rice salad is a joy. Use long-grain white rice, basmati, Arborio, or even sushi rice. More important than the variety is that the rice not be overcooked or mushy. The grains should be firm and separate. The best way to achieve this is to boil the rice like pasta, in lots of water, rather than steam it.

2 cups Arborio rice

1 shallot, finely chopped

2 tablespoons fresh lemon juice, or to taste

1 tablespoon white wine vinegar

Salt and pepper

1 teaspoon Dijon mustard

About ¼ cup olive oil

1 tablespoon each finely chopped parsley, chives, chervil, mint, and dill

Bring 4 quarts of lightly salted water to a boil in a big pot. Add the rice and boil briskly until the grains are ever-so-slightly al dente, about 15 minutes. Drain the rice in a colander, then spread it out on a baking sheet to cool.

Macerate the shallot in the lemon juice, vinegar, and salt to taste for about 10 minutes. Stir in the mustard to dissolve, then whisk in ¼ cup olive oil.

When the rice is cool, put it in a wide salad bowl, fluff it up with your fingers, and season lightly with salt and pepper. Pour over the vinaigrette and toss lightly.

Just before serving, chop the herbs. Sprinkle the herbs over the rice and gently mix them in. Taste and correct the seasonings, adding salt, lemon juice, and olive oil if necessary. Transfer to a serving platter.

{VARIATION} RICE SALAD LUNCH
With the addition of chicken or shrimp, a few dressed tomatoes and cucumbers, and quartered soft-center hard-cooked eggs, this rice salad can become a perfect summer main course.

Lemon Verbena Bavarian Cream

The leaves of lemon verbena make a fine herbal tea or tisane, but its delicate light lemony, herby scent is excellent for flavoring desserts as well. Although fresh lemon verbena is wonderful, dried lemon verbena works well too. Lacking either of these, you could steep branches of lemon thyme or rose-scented geranium in the milk.

The point is to steep the floral herbs in the warmed milk just long enough to impart a subtle flavor.

4 cups organic whole milk
2 cups loosely packed lemon
   verbena leaves, fresh or dried
½ cup sugar
¼ teaspoon salt

2 tablespoons powdered gelatin,
   softened in 2 tablespoons cold
   water
Artisanal lavender honey
   (optional)

Heat the milk in a heavy-bottomed saucepan to just under a boil, then turn off the heat. Plunge the lemon verbena leaves into the milk and let them steep for 5 to 10 minutes. Taste to gauge the intensity of flavor.

Strain the milk into a big bowl. Whisk in the sugar, salt, and softened gelatin and combine well. Cool the mixture to room temperature, and pour into a 1-quart mold. Or, if you happen to have a decorative Jell-O mold, now's the time to use it. Cover and refrigerate the Bavarian mixture for at least 4 hours, or overnight for a firmer cream.

To serve, invert the mold onto a platter (it should slide out easily). With a large flat spoon, make thick slices. Drizzle honey sparingly over the cream, if you like.

Fall Menus

menu eleven
COOKING AMERICAN
Shrimp "Cocktail" in a Glass

Peppery Chicken Wings

Fried Green Tomatoes

Spicy Cabbage Slaw

Scalloped Corn

Molasses Pecan Squares

menu twelve
FLATBREAD WISDOM
Rosemary and Scallion Focaccia

Sweet Pepper and Cauliflower Salad

Raviolone with Butternut Squash in Butter and Sage

Figs, Grapes, and Vin Santo

menu thirteen
RIPENESS OF RED CHILES
Platter of Jicama, Avocado, Radishes, and Oranges

Slow-Cooked Carne Adovada with Hominy

Mexican Chocolate Ice Cream

menu fourteen
NEARLY VEGETARIAN
Vegetables à la Grecque

Wild Mushroom Ragout with Ziti

Chard and Ricotta Tart

menu fifteen
THE TROUBLE WITH HAM
Hors d'Oeuvres Variés: Roasted Beet Salad, Julienned Carrot Salad,
    and Leeks Vinaigrette

Petit Salé with Braised Cabbage

Quince Slices (and Beyond)

Walnuts and a Few Cheeses

Cooking American

Shrimp "Cocktail" in a Glass
Peppery Chicken Wings
Fried Green Tomatoes
Spicy Cabbage Slaw
Scalloped Corn
Molasses Pecan Squares

When I cook American food, it's a little like when I conjure up my inner Italian or inner Spaniard—it's a bit of a masquerade. If I crave American food, I have to go into my pretend-citizen mode. It's as if I'm doomed to travel the world in search of my real culture.

It's not that I'm not American, it's that I grew up in Ohio, where there's no discernible regional cuisine—unless you count funnel cakes. Owing to that particular geographical spot and era, I gained my knowledge of American cooking through other people's reminiscences. And the occasional foray into James Beard. There's something odd about having nostalgia for something I never really knew.

It wasn't until I got out into the world that I learned about corn bread and gumbo, Indian pudding, chicken and dumplings, sweet pickles, and fried green tomatoes.

There's a lot of traditional American cooking with real depth. Let's never get so cool that we write off the familiar. In any discussion of food, regional cuisine has value, no matter where the region. Especially in late summer and early autumn, the American bug bites. I might go elsewhere in my culinary travels in the winter, but at harvesttime, I want the last of the tomatoes, one more hit of good corn and cabbage, fresh American comfort food.

Shrimp "Cocktail" in a Glass

Among the best shrimp I ever tasted were from those little restaurants along the docks in Veracruz, where you used to get freshly boiled shrimp in the shell, to be eaten with salt and lime. They also served a magnificent shellfish creation made with all manner of shrimp, oysters, and crabmeat mixed with onion, chopped tomato, chiles, and cilantro. It was topped with a soupy tomato salsa and served in an ice cream soda glass. That's the origin of this recipe, a better version of the all-too-often bland American-style shrimp cocktail.

Use fresh shrimp that you boil yourself, and take care not to overcook them.

2 dozen medium shrimp,
   shell on

FOR THE BOIL
1 tablespoon salt
1 bay leaf
3 garlic cloves, sliced
1 teaspoon black peppercorns
1 teaspoon coriander seeds
1 teaspoon fennel seeds
1 teaspoon red pepper flakes
4 thyme sprigs

FOR THE SAUCE
3 scallions, minced
1 large tomato, diced small
Salt and pepper
2 teaspoons finely diced jalapeño
   or serrano chile
2 to 3 tablespoons chopped parsley
2 to 3 tablespoons chopped
   cilantro
Juice of 2 limes
2 cups homemade or high-quality
   bottled tomato juice

Peel and devein the shrimp; keep them cold.

Bring 8 cups water to a boil in a large pot. Add the salt, bay leaf, garlic, black peppercorns, coriander seeds, fennel seeds, red pepper flakes, and thyme. Simmer for 5 minutes.

Toss the shrimp into the pot, bring back to a boil, and cook for 1 minute. Scoop the shrimp out and lay them on a platter to cool.

To make the sauce, put the scallions and tomato in a bowl, and salt and pepper them well. Add the diced chile, chopped parsley and cilantro, lime juice, and tomato juice and stir it all together. Taste for seasoning.

Fill each of 6 short thick-walled glasses with plenty of sauce, top each with 4 peeled shrimp, and refrigerate until well chilled. Or, better, stick the glasses into a big bowl of crushed ice and serve from there.

Peppery Chicken Wings

There's something wonderful about a big pile of wings for a casual supper. Remove the wing tips (save them for stock), so that what you're serving is the meatier part of the wing. You can use the same seasoning and technique for chicken thighs if you prefer.

5 pounds chicken wings, wing tips
   removed
Salt and pepper
2 teaspoons ground allspice
¼ teaspoon ground cloves

1 teaspoon cayenne
1 tablespoon sweet paprika
4 garlic cloves, smashed to a paste
   with a little salt
3 tablespoons olive oil

Lay the chicken wings out on a baking sheet and season well with salt and pepper. Transfer the wings to a big mixing bowl, add all the other ingredients, and give the wings a massage. Refrigerate for at least an hour, or as long as overnight.

Preheat the oven to 375°F. Put the wings in a roasting pan or baking sheet in one layer. Roast, uncovered, until nicely browned and crisp, about 1 hour. You can eat them hot, at room temperature, or cold.

Fried Green Tomatoes

The end of summer is the time for those green tomatoes that will never ripen. You can pickle them, or turn them into green tomato pie. I like them best fried.

4 to 6 green (unripe) tomatoes
Salt and pepper
2 cups all-purpose flour

1 cup fine yellow cornmeal
1 teaspoon cayenne
Olive or vegetable oil for frying

Cut the tomatoes into ½-inch-thick slices and season on both sides with salt and pepper.

Mix the flour and cornmeal in a pie pan, add the cayenne and a generous amount of salt and pepper, and stir well.

Heat ¼ inch of oil in a large cast-iron skillet over medium-high heat. When the oil is hot, working in batches, dip the slices of green tomato into the flour mixture, turning to coat both sides, and carefully lay them in the pan; make only one layer. Cook the tomato slices on one side until they're lightly browned, 2 to 3 minutes, then turn and lightly brown the second side. Sprinkle them with salt as soon as they come out of the pan. Keep them warm in a low oven while you fry another batch. Drain on paper towels.

Spicy Cabbage Slaw

Of the zillions of versions of coleslaw, I'm not a big fan of the sweet ones, or the mayonnaise ones either. This recipe is more like a refreshing cabbage salad.

1 small firm green cabbage,
   cored and shredded
1 small red onion, very thinly
   sliced

1 jalapeño or serrano chile,
   finely chopped
Juice of 3 limes, or to taste
Salt and pepper

Put the cabbage, onion, chile, and lime juice in a bowl, season with salt and pepper, and toss well. Cover and refrigerate for at least an hour.

After an hour, the cabbage will have wilted slightly. Taste for salt and lime juice, adjust the seasonings, and serve.

Scalloped Corn

This old-fashioned corn dish combines the appeal of creamed corn with corn pudding.

2 tablespoons butter, plus more for buttering the dish and topping	Pinch of cayenne
1 small yellow onion, finely diced	1½ cups half-and-half
Salt and pepper	Kernels from 6 ears sweet corn (about 3 cups)
2 tablespoons all-purpose flour	2 egg yolks
	½ cup fresh bread crumbs

Preheat the oven to 375°F. Butter a 10-inch baking dish.

Melt the 2 tablespoons butter over medium heat in a medium skillet, and soften the onion with a little salt, about 5 minutes. Sprinkle in the flour, season with salt and pepper and cayenne, and stir well with a wooden spoon.

Slowly add the half-and-half and stir well as the sauce thickens. Add the corn kernels and simmer for 2 minutes. Taste and adjust the seasoning. Remove from the heat.

Beat the egg yolks in a small bowl, and stir into the corn mixture.

Pour the corn mixture into the baking dish. Scatter the bread crumbs over the top and dot with butter. Bake for about 30 minutes, or until golden.

Molasses Pecan Squares

Molasses is a classic American ingredient, and so are pecans. Here they make a dessert that is a little like gingerbread.

8 tablespoons (1 stick) butter, softened, plus more for buttering the dish
1 cup packed dark brown sugar
2 eggs, separated
2 tablespoons molasses
½ teaspoon vanilla extract

½ cup all-purpose flour
1 teaspoon baking powder
½ teaspoon salt
½ cup chopped pecans, plus a handful of whole pecans for topping

Preheat the oven to 375°F. Butter and flour a 9-inch-square baking dish. Cream the 8 tablespoons butter and sugar in a mixing bowl. (An electric mixer is helpful.) Add the egg yolks, molasses, and vanilla and beat well.

Sift the flour with the baking powder and salt, and add to the mixing bowl, stirring well. Stir in the chopped pecans.

In another bowl, beat the egg whites until stiff. Gently fold them into the batter.

Spread the batter in the dish, and sprinkle the whole pecans over the top. Bake for 35 to 40 minutes. Check for doneness with a kitchen knife; when it comes out dry, the dessert is done. Cool in the pan and cut into 3-inch squares.

Flatbread Wisdom

Rosemary and Scallion Focaccia
Sweet Pepper and Cauliflower Salad
Raviolone with Butternut Squash in Butter and Sage
Figs, Grapes, and Vin Santo

Liguria Bakery has stood as a hole-in-the-wall temple to focaccia in San Francisco's North Beach for a hundred years. Its premise is simple: focaccia and nothing but. I love their white scallion, and their red, stained with a thin tomato sauce. Although the bakery is open seven days a week, you'd better notice the tiny type that reads "Closed early if sold out." They do, and they do, so get there early. You can have your focaccia in two sizes, a whole tray or a half tray. If you buy a whole tray, they'll cut it in half all the same, wrap it in classic white butcher paper, and tie it with pure white butcher string. And you leave with that package under your arm one lucky customer.

Once you learn to make focaccia and it becomes part of your repertoire, making it becomes second nature when you're inviting people over or making dinner for the family. What makes it relatively easy is the simple yeast dough—just a soft dough that's enriched with olive oil—that you pat into a baking sheet and let rise.

Just before baking, you add the toppings, whether rosemary leaves and salt, stewed onions and scallions, thin tomato sauce and anchovies, or, for a spectacular autumn focaccia, wine grapes. After you've applied the topping, you delicately dimple the dough. Pushing your fingertips into the soft dough is primal and satisfying.

When it's baked, the focaccia has its characteristic crisped exterior. Inside, it's soft, rich, and savory.

Rosemary and Scallion Focaccia

Focaccia dough works best if you mix it the night before. One recipe will make a lovely flat bread about 10 by 15 inches, the size of a standard baking sheet.

If you want it thinner, of course, you'll use a bigger sheet; thicker?—use a smaller baking sheet. Focaccia, and its French cousin *fougasse,* are often made free-form on a baking sheet, which is also a very nice idea. Unlike pizza, focaccia needs to rise to achieve the proper texture.

For a simple yet voluptuous first course, I serve freshly baked focaccia with a platter of prosciutto, a bowl of olives, a little mild white cheese such as ricotta salata, and the Sweet Pepper and Cauliflower Salad.

1½ cups lukewarm water
1 tablespoon active dry yeast
3 cups all-purpose flour,
   plus extra for sprinkling
2 teaspoons fine sea salt

½ cup olive oil, plus extra
   for drizzling
½ cup roughly chopped scallions
1 tablespoon roughly chopped
   rosemary
Coarse salt for sprinkling

Put ½ cup of the warm water in a mixing bowl. Add the yeast and 3 tablespoons of the flour and stir together. Let the mixture sit until it gets bubbly, about 5 minutes.

Add the remaining 1 cup water, the rest of the flour, the salt, and olive oil. Stir with a wooden spoon until the mixture gathers into a rough, sticky mass. Sprinkle the dough lightly with a little more flour, and knead the dough in the bowl for a minute or so. Then turn the dough out onto the table and just give it a couple of turns with your hands.

Lightly oil a bowl large enough to contain the dough—it will rise a little bit in the fridge. Cover tightly with plastic wrap and refrigerate overnight.

{CONTINUED}

The next day, remove the dough from the refrigerator and pat and press it into a generously oiled baking sheet. It might spring back a bit. Allow this to happen, and wait a few minutes. It will eventually relax and become more malleable.

Now the focaccia needs to rise in a warm place for about an hour, covered well with plastic wrap or wax paper.

Preheat the oven to 400° F. Scatter the scallions and rosemary evenly across the top of the dough and drizzle with olive oil. Poke little dimples evenly over the top of the focaccia, and sprinkle with coarse sea salt. Bake for 25 to 30 minutes, until it's nicely browned on top and the bottom seems done. Cool to room temperature, if you can wait.

{OTHER TASTY TOPPINGS}

Instead of rosemary and scallions, sprinkle the dough with 2 teaspoons crushed fennel seeds, some red pepper flakes, and a generous amount of freshly ground black pepper. Or poke green olives or chopped pancetta into the dimples on top of the focaccia.

{VARIATION} WINE GRAPE FOCACCIA

In the autumn, a wonderful sweet and savory focaccia can be made with ripe wine grapes and caramelized onions. Replace the scallions with a cup of red onion caramelized in a little olive oil with salt and pepper, and poke wine grapes into the dimples you've made on the surface of the dough (you could also use fresh table grapes). Top it with the rosemary and salt.

Sweet Pepper and Cauliflower Salad

This is a version of the Italian giardiniera that's typically made with any number of vegetables in a pleasantly tangy dressing.

1 small cauliflower
½ pound yellow wax beans,
   cut into 1-inch lengths
½ pound green beans,
   cut into 1-inch lengths
1 large shallot, finely diced
2 tablespoons red wine vinegar
1 tablespoon sherry vinegar
Salt and pepper
1 garlic clove, smashed to a paste
   with a little salt

1 teaspoon Dijon mustard
2 teaspoons roughly chopped
   capers
¼ cup olive oil
1 large sweet red pepper,
   cut into ½-inch dice
1 large sweet yellow pepper,
   cut into ½-inch dice
Basil and parsley leaves for
   garnish

Cut the cauliflower into the smallest florets possible. Bring a medium pot of salted water to a boil. Add the cauliflower and cook for a minute, then remove and spread it on a platter to cool to room temperature.

Do the same with the beans, though they might need a minute longer to cook. Let cool.

To make the dressing, in a small bowl, combine the shallot with the vinegars and a little salt and pepper. Let it sit for 5 minutes, then stir in the garlic, mustard, and capers. Whisk in the olive oil and check the seasonings.

Put the cauliflower, beans, and peppers in a large bowl. Season with salt and pepper and toss well. Now add the dressing and toss again to coat. Let the vegetables macerate for at least 15 minutes, or up to an hour.

Scatter basil and parsley leaves over the top.

Raviolone with Butternut Squash in Butter and Sage

Fresh egg pasta is surprisingly easy to make, and the results are well worth it. In Italy, these raviolone would be stuffed with zucca, a tasty pumpkin, but here, a better choice is a firm-fleshed winter squash like butternut, because our pumpkin can be watery.

Both the filling and pasta dough can be made many hours ahead, say in the morning. Then roll out the pasta and stuff the raviolone an hour before the meal. Since raviolone are large, triangular ravioli, you need only about 3 per person. Use the same dough to make smaller ravioli if you'd prefer.

SERVES 4 TO 6

FOR THE PASTA

2 cups all-purpose flour

4 large eggs

Pinch of salt

2 tablespoons olive oil

FOR THE FILLING

1 large butternut squash, about 2 pounds

Salt and pepper

2 tablespoons olive oil

½ cup freshly grated pecorino romano

Grated zest of 1 lemon

1 teaspoon red pepper flakes

Nutmeg for grating

FOR THE SAUCE

4 tablespoons butter

A small bunch of sage (about 6 leaves per person)

Salt and pepper

1 garlic clove, smashed to a paste with a little salt

Juice of ½ lemon

A chunk of aged Parmigiano or ricotta salata for shaving

To make the pasta dough, put the flour in a bowl. In another bowl, beat the eggs with the salt and olive oil. Pour the eggs into the flour and stir until the dough comes together. It'll look a little raggedy, but that's fine.

Dump the dough out onto a lightly floured counter and knead for a few minutes, until it looks soft and smooth. Wrap the dough in plastic and set aside to rest for at least 1 hour, or up to several hours. (This allows the dough to relax and become stretchable, and the flour to absorb all the moisture.)

Meanwhile, to make the filling, preheat the oven to 375°F. Slice the squash lengthwise in half, scoop out the seeds, and put on a baking sheet, skin side up. Bake for about an hour, or until the flesh is tender when tested with a fork. Set aside to cool.

Scoop out the flesh of the squash and put it in a bowl. Season well with salt and pepper. Add the rest of the filling ingredients, including a little grated nutmeg, and stir well. Taste and adjust the seasonings—it should be rather highly seasoned to balance the sweetness of the squash.

Divide the pasta dough into 4 pieces, and flatten each piece. Roll each piece through your hand-cranked pasta maker all the way to the next-to-thinnest setting, placing the pieces on a floured counter as you work. You'll end up with 4 sheets of pasta about 4 inches wide and 16 inches long.

To assemble the raviolone, cut 1 pasta sheet into 4 equal pieces. Put 2 tablespoons of the filling slightly off center on each square. With a pastry brush or fingertip, lightly moisten the edges with water, then fold each square over into a triangle. Repeat with the remaining 3 sheets. Pick up the triangles and place them in a single layer on a lightly floured towel. Cover loosely with plastic wrap and refrigerate, or leave at cool room temperature for up to 1 hour until ready to cook.

{CONTINUED}

Put two large wide pots of well-salted water on the stove and bring to a boil. Add half the raviolone to the boiling water in each pot and cook for 3 to 4 minutes. To check for doneness, remove 1 triangle, put it on a cutting board, and slice off a corner of pasta to taste. When it's done, with a big spider or slotted spoon, gently lift the cooked pasta from the water and put it on a warm deep platter.

Quickly make the sauce by heating the butter in a small skillet over medium-high heat. When the butter is melted, toss in the sage leaves, roughly chopped if you wish, season with salt and pepper, and let the sage sizzle a bit. Stir in the garlic, without letting it brown, then turn off the heat, squeeze in the lemon juice, and stir well. Pour the sauce over the raviolone. With a vegetable peeler, shave the cheese over the platter, and serve immediately.

Figs, Grapes, and Vin Santo

Early autumn is your last chance for the sun-ripened fresh figs you find at a farmers' market or pick off a friend's venerable tree. Wash a couple of fig leaves, if you're lucky enough to get them, lay them on a platter, and pile high with juicy, ripe figs.

The problem with grapes is that they are too much with us, imported from South America in all seasons, and usually not very tasty. Their very ubiquity has turned us away from the delights of table grapes in the peak of their season, but every region in this country has its own varieties of grape—the glorious last gasp of summer.

I particularly favor big fat floral muscats. I also like muscadines and scuppernongs in the South, the sweeter varieties of Concords in the Northeast, and the little green grapes with a bronze blush, inexplicably called Bronx, that we get on the West Coast. I love the shimmery dusting of fall grapes that almost look as if they've been sugared. After tasting such beauties, you'll never be able to look those one-note supermarket grapes in the eye again.

Just put big bunches of grapes on a platter and pour little glasses of vin santo, a sweet fortified wine that's aged in barrels like sherry. Its mellow flavors develop under the eaves in many a Tuscan attic, warmed by the afternoon sun.

Ripeness of Red Chiles

Platter of Jicama, Avocado, Radishes, and Oranges
Slow-Cooked Carne Adovada with Hominy
Mexican Chocolate Ice Cream

When I lived in New Mexico, I knew lots of people who grew their own red chiles, but hardly anybody could grind their own. So what you'd do is make an appointment with the chile grinder, and you'd take your dried chiles out to his place in the sparse, rocky Badlands. As soon as you arrived, he'd lead you out to an immaculate little barn, empty except for a mechanical grinder in the middle of the room. He'd power it by backing his tractor up to the barn and stretching a belt through the window from the tractor to the grinder. The aroma of those chiles as they were ground was so sweet, so pungent, and so red.

The old man and his wife lived alone out there, and he had been a chile grinder forever. When he was done, he unhooked the belt from the grinder, pulled his tractor away, swept out the barn, and went back inside his little house.

So many things can take me back to the aroma of that little barn: opening a jar of piment d'Espelette, the dried French Basque chiles, or a tin of smoky Spanish pimentón. If I get homesick enough, I'll ask a friend to send me some new-crop red chiles.

ESTEEMING THE CHILE PEPPER

It was easy to fall in love with chiles. My initiation was with a bowl of spicy dumplings. The dumplings were swimming in a steaming sea of chicken broth, showered with an enormous handful of just chopped green chiles, scallions, and Chinese parsley. The first spoonful produced a scalp-tingling glow, and a craving was born.

Early travels to Mexico only fanned the fire, as did trips to southeast Asia. It didn't hurt that my cooking pal Niloufer was always making incendiary green chutneys and serving me extraordinary piquant trotters with lentils. In Berkeley, there was (and still is) a Thai temple where food concessionaires gathered outside on Sundays; the food and attendant socializing were as much an attraction as the service inside. I loved to go there for an ultra-zingy green papaya salad, laced with pounded tiny chiles. Before long, I found myself living in Santa Fe, feasting on fresh roasted green chiles in the fall and dried red-chile-sauced tamales year-round. And I confess I rather like the look of dried chiles hanging from rafters and doorways.

People think chile peppers are just *hot,* but they're much more. They have a vegetal sweetness, a richness. There's a reason for that red sweetness: the chiles are red when they're harvested because they're allowed to ripen on the plant beyond the sharpness of their green pepper state.

Chiles are native to the Americas—the diminutive chile tepin grows wild still. But these days many varieties of spicy-hot capsicum pepper are grown all around the globe and featured in countless cuisines. The use of chiles can be quite restrained or quite assertive, depending on the whims of the cook. I'm always sneaking a bit into my cooking to heighten flavor and add brightness, even in delicate egg or pasta dishes.

It's encouraging to note that fresh chiles are more and more available at supermarkets. Now you can almost always find fat jalapeños, slim serranos, little red Fresnos, pale yellow wax peppers, and dark glossy poblanos.

Except for poblanos, which must be roasted and peeled, they're all good finely diced, chopped, or slivered. Of course, other varieties of fresh hot chiles can be found in Latino, Indian, and Chinese groceries.

Larger leathery ruddy red dried chiles—such as New Mexico, ancho, and guajillo—are the ones to use for sauces, marinades, stews, and soups. Toasted lightly and seeds removed, they are then simmered before being blended into a paste. These can also be ground into a fine red chile powder, or coarsely crushed to make *caribe,* medium-size chile flakes.

Slipping a few chiles into the suitcase has become my habitual travel insurance. When I visited my old friend Sue, a larger-than-life actress in Los Angeles, she recoiled dramatically when I brought chiles to her table. Little by little, I wore her down. Now she proudly tells me she always chops up a jalapeño for her breakfast eggs. Forevermore beholden to the craving, she is happily spreading the gospel, too.

Platter of Jicama, Avocado, Radishes, and Oranges

This is typical street food in Mexico, sold in market stalls, especially from fruit vendors, who cut up papayas, pineapples, oranges, and cucumbers and serve them with salt, chile, and a squeeze of lime. Beautiful powdered spicy red *chile molido*—ground chile—is mixed with salt and sprinkled over the fruit.

For me, it's a short leap from that cart to the kitchen counter, where a platter of fresh fruits and vegetables translates perfectly to a stand-up appetizer with drinks. Use any combination that appeals to you. For the best red chile powder, visit your Latino or Indian grocery.

1 small jicama, peeled and
    thinly sliced

2 avocados, peeled, pitted,
    and sliced

1 large bunch radishes, trimmed

3 navel oranges, sliced into thick
    rounds

2 small cucumbers, peeled and
    quartered lengthwise

A few Mexican or Key limes

Salt

Good-quality red chile powder

Arrange all the fruits and vegetables beautifully on one huge platter (or on a banana leaf if you happen to have one handy), and surround with halved limes.

In a small serving bowl, mix equal parts salt and chile powder. Or do this to taste—you can make the mix saltier or spicier. Dip a lime half in the chile mix, rub on the spices, and squeeze the lime juice over the fruit and vegetables.

Slow-Cooked Carne Adovada with Hominy

The New Mexican way with pork is a celebration of dried red chiles. Basically, you soften the long, leathery chile peppers by simmering them in a little water, puree them into an intense paste, and smother the meat in this marinade. Then the meat, the *picante* marinade, and the slow, slow cooking result in the best pulled pork you've ever had. Now, I'm not putting down anybody else's barbecue, and I'm not even saying this is barbecue. This is quite simply the pork of your dreams. SERVES 4 TO 6

6 ounces dried New Mexico
   red chiles

2 tablespoons lard or vegetable oil

1 large onion, finely diced

Salt and pepper

6 garlic cloves, roughly chopped

1 teaspoon coriander seeds,
   toasted and ground

1 teaspoon cumin seeds,
   toasted and ground

1 bay leaf

3 pounds boneless pork shoulder,
   left whole or cut into large
   chunks

Hominy (page 188)

Rinse and dry the chiles, then toast them in a dry cast-iron pan over medium heat until they puff a bit and become fragrant, 2 to 3 minutes. Cut the chiles lengthwise in half and remove the stems and seeds.

Put the chiles in a small pot of water and bring to a boil. Simmer for about 5 minutes. Let the chiles cool in the liquid. Puree the chiles with a cup of their cooking liquid in a blender until smooth.

Heat the lard or oil in a large skillet over medium heat. Add the onion, season with salt and pepper, and cook for about 5 minutes. No color, no browning. Add the garlic, coriander, cumin, and bay leaf, then add the chile puree and a little salt and simmer for another 5 minutes. Cool the mixture. (You can do this well ahead if you wish.)

{CONTINUED}

Preheat the oven to 350°F. Put the pork in a low roasting pan or a heavy-bottomed ovenproof pot and season generously with salt and pepper. Pour the chile sauce over the pork and mix well to coat. Cover tightly with a lid or foil.

Bake the pork for 1½ to 2 hours, until the meat is quite tender and falling apart. (This dish can be made a day or many hours ahead and reheated.)

Serve the carne adovada in shallow soup bowls with a big spoonful of the steaming-hot hominy.

Hominy

Hominy or pozole, like dried beans, should be soaked overnight. Then it can be simmered for an hour and a half or so, unattended, at any time during the day you are serving it. As it slowly cooks, the hominy perfumes the kitchen with its sweet aroma. Freshly cooked hominy has a corny flavor and a pearly texture that you can't get from canned. It's perfect as a starch to accompany a spicy pork stew and it's delicious in many soups as well.

1 pound dried hominy, soaked
   overnight in water to cover
4 quarts water
1 teaspoon salt, or to taste

1 small onion, halved and stuck
   with a clove
6 garlic cloves
2 medium carrots, peeled and
   chunked

Drain the hominy, rinse, and put in a soup pot. Cover with the water, add the salt, onion, garlic, and carrots, and bring to a boil. Reduce the heat and simmer for 1½ to 2 hours, until the kernels have swelled and softened. Discard the aromatics. Taste for salt, and add a bit more if needed. Serve immediately, or reheat when ready.

Mexican Chocolate Ice Cream

Mexican chocolate, available here in thick round tablets, is rather granular, with a certain rustic quality—you can still taste the toasty cacao pods. It's usually flavored with cinnamon, and often nutmeg or allspice, too.

If you can't find Mexican chocolate, use bittersweet instead and add a 2-inch length of cinnamon stick, a couple of cloves, and a pinch each of nutmeg and allspice to the warm milk; discard the spices once the mixture is cool.

3 cups whole milk	**¾ cup sugar**
8 ounces Mexican chocolate	**½ teaspoon salt**

Warm the milk in a medium saucepan. Grate the chocolate coarsely, then stir it into the warm milk. Add the sugar and salt and stir over low heat for about 5 minutes, until everything is well dissolved. Let cool.

Churn the mixture in your ice cream maker for 15 to 20 minutes, then transfer to a container and freeze for at least 1 hour.

Nearly Vegetarian

Vegetables à la Grecque
Wild Mushroom Ragout with Ziti
Chard and Ricotta Tart

Sometimes I think I could easily be a vegetarian save for a few small exceptions—like pork, for example. There are all sorts of what I like to think of as situation vegetarians: you have your bacon vegetarians, and your chicken vegetarians, and your fish vegetarians.

I even know a vegetarian who eats hamburgers while traveling because he says it's just easier. Upon his return from a trip, he goes back to being a vegetarian. When Alain Passard announced he was embracing vegetarianism at his three-star restaurant Arpège in Paris, he got a lot of press. But this big deal turned out to mean no red meat on the menu—just birds and fish. At Arpège, though, I had the most memorable plate of beets, caramelized with onions and served warm.

There's a whole awful tradition of making vegetarian ingredients masquerade as something else. In the 1970s, health-food nuts were always cooking things like lentil loaf and vegetable protein cutlets, with the intent of making you think you were eating something meaty. Today the final insult is tofurkey—it is demeaning to the tofu, and it's demeaning to the turkey.

At home, I often cook meals that turn out almost inadvertently to be vegetarian. But I also like cooking a vegetable stew with a little bit of meat—bacon, or *petit salé* (see page 204), for example—added for flavor. I also love the traditional Chinese dish of spicy tofu with meat sauce.

We think of summer as the season of the vegetable. But when you get to autumn, there is a whole new basket of vegetables waiting for you: bitter chicories, cauliflower, winter squashes, and wild mushrooms in full force. It's truly the last glory time before the weather starts turning cold for good.

Vegetables à la Grecque

The Greek origins of this manner of cooking vegetables are lost in the dim mists of history, but look in any French cookbook, and you'll find a recipe for all kinds of vegetables prepared à la grecque: artichokes, zucchini, celery and celery root, fennel, carrots, onions, cardoons, mushrooms. It's a straightforward technique well suited to Mediterranean vegetables, or almost any vegetable for that matter. You simmer white wine, olive oil, and herbs to make a tasty bath for whichever vegetables you prefer.

The ultimate result is a platter of delicious lightly pickled vegetables, which can be cooked ahead and served at room temperature, giving them an admirable versatility. They can accompany any main course or, paired with a few olives, a piece of feta cheese, and good bread, make a meal.

FOR THE POACHING LIQUID
2 cups dry white wine
2 cups olive oil
2 cups water
2 teaspoons salt, or to taste
1 teaspoon coriander seeds
1 teaspoon fennel seeds
1 teaspoon black peppercorns
1 bay leaf
1 small bunch thyme
6 garlic cloves, thickly sliced
1 small lemon, sliced
2 tablespoons white wine vinegar

FOR THE VEGETABLES
12 boiling onions, red or white
6 medium carrots, peeled and halved lengthwise
2 small fennel bulbs, trimmed and cut into small wedges (or use celery hearts)
2 medium zucchini, cut into thick batons

To make the poaching liquid, combine all the ingredients in a wide nonreactive (enamel or stainless steel) heavy-bottomed pot and bring to a boil.

{CONTINUED}

Reduce the heat and simmer for about 5 minutes. Taste and adjust for salt. It should be well seasoned, as this bath will flavor the vegetables.

Some people dump all the vegetables into the pot at once, but they're a bit hard to keep track of that way, since each has a different cooking time. The way I learned it is to cook the vegetables separately, to make sure none is overcooked. The goal is tender, not mushy, vegetables.

Start with the onions. Simmer them gently until easily pierced with a skewer, about 10 minutes. Remove from the poaching liquid with a slotted spoon and let them cool on a plate. Continue with the other vegetables, counting on about 5 minutes for the carrots and fennel, and about 3 minutes for the zucchini.

Strain and cool the poaching liquid.

Put the vegetables in a deep wide dish and pour the cooled liquid over them. Let them sit in the liquid for at least a few hours, or refrigerate overnight.

When you're ready to serve, remove the vegetables to a platter and spoon a little of the poaching liquid over the top. Serve at room temperature.

FORAGING FOR WILD MUSHROOMS

Hunting wild mushrooms is a thrill. Once you've learned (from a legitimate mushroom authority) how to distinguish two or three varieties, it's the best kind of shopping experience. One of the first times I went hunting for porcini was with a really good mushroom hunter. We drove four or five hours to get to the forest where he claimed the mushrooms were. We found ourselves deep in the woods but we saw only pine needles on the forest floor. Then he showed me how to read the needles. Beneath a vague bump, trying to poke its head up, was a fat *Boletus edulis!* I felt pretty lucky. Usually, you can never ask a mushroom hunter for his favorite spots, because he'll tell you the wrong place every time.

The varieties of wild mushroom that typically come to market in the autumn are chanterelles; black trumpets, sometimes called black chanterelles; yellowfoot; hedgehog; and, if you're really lucky, porcini. It's excellent to have many different kinds of mushroom in your stew, but one variety will do as well. And even if you have no access to fresh wild mushrooms, you can make a satisfying ragout with cultivated varieties such as portobello, cremini, or a combination of button mushrooms and a little dried wild mushroom powder.

Wild mushrooms will range from quite muddy to beautifully dry, but either way, they need a bit of prep to ready them for cooking. Wild mushrooms should be picked over and trimmed with a paring knife, removing soft spots, sticks, and wormholes. It's better to trim them first, then determine if they need a rinse. Generally speaking, mushrooms and water don't mix. Only if your mushrooms are full of dirt and debris should you dunk them quickly: Fill a bowl with lukewarm water, plunge the mushrooms into the warm bath for 2 seconds, and immediately remove them to dry on a towel. Cultivated button mushrooms and cremini are sometimes a little gritty; rinse them quickly under running warm water, in a colander. Portobellos and oyster mushrooms usually just need to be trimmed.

Wild Mushroom Ragout with Ziti

Although many vegetarians I know are understandably tired of pasta, this deeply satisfying autumnal dish isn't so much a pasta as a rich mushroom stew that would be just as wonderful with warm polenta, steamed rice, or other grains.

FOR THE MUSHROOM RAGOUT

¼ cup olive oil

1 large onion, finely diced

Salt and pepper

2 pounds wild or cultivated
  mushrooms, cleaned and sliced

3 garlic cloves, smashed to a paste
  with a little salt

1 teaspoon finely chopped thyme

2 teaspoons finely chopped sage

½ teaspoon red pepper flakes

2 tablespoons tomato paste

1 tablespoon all-purpose flour

2 cups Porcini Mushroom Broth
  (recipe follows), hot, or as
  needed

1 pound long ziti

2 tablespoons olive oil or butter

2 garlic cloves

Salt and pepper

2 tablespoons chopped parsley

To prepare the ragout, in a large skillet, heat 2 tablespoons of the olive oil over high heat. Add the onion and cook, stirring well, until it begins to brown. Lower the heat to medium, season the onions with salt and pepper, and continue stirring until nicely caramelized, about 5 minutes. Remove the onion to a small bowl. Return the pan to the heat, add the remaining 2 tablespoons olive oil, and turn the heat to high. Add the mushrooms, stirring well to coat with oil. Keep the heat high and sauté the mushrooms until they brown lightly. If juices accumulate in the pan, pour them off and reserve.

Season the mushrooms with salt and pepper, add the garlic, thyme, sage, and pepper flakes, and stir well. Reduce the heat to medium, add the caramelized onion and the tomato paste, and stir well to coat the mushrooms and to dry the mixture slightly. Cook for another 2 minutes, stirring.

{CONTINUED}

Sprinkle the flour over the mixture and stir it in. Ladle in 1 cup of the hot mushroom broth, stirring well as the mixture thickens. Add another cup of hot broth and let the ragout cook for another 5 minutes. If it's too thin, cook it a bit longer; if too thick, add a bit more broth. Taste for seasoning. (The ragout can be made a few hours ahead and reheated.)

To cook the pasta, bring a large pot of salted water to a boil. Break the ziti into 6-inch lengths (or use cut ziti). Boil the pasta for about 10 minutes, or until on the firm side of al dente.

When the noodles are almost cooked, warm the olive oil or butter in a large wide skillet. Put in the garlic and stir; don't let it brown. Add salt and pepper and turn off the heat.

Drain the pasta, add to the skillet along with the parsley, and mix well. Transfer the pasta to a warm serving bowl. Put the hot mushroom ragout in another serving bowl, and bring them both to the table.

Porcini Mushroom Broth

Put 3 cups water in a saucepan and add a bay leaf, a few slices of dried porcini mushrooms or 2 teaspoons dry porcini powder (see below), half a small onion, 1 small celery stalk, and a small carrot, peeled and chopped. Bring to a boil, then lower to a simmer and cook for 20 to 30 minutes; strain.

{VARIATION} DRY PORCINI POWDER

Porcini powder is available at specialty shops, but it's easy to make your own, to add intensity to the mushroom ragout or many other sauces or dishes. Dried porcini can sometimes be sandy. So, to get rid of any grit, soak a handful of them briefly in warm water, then blot them very well in a towel, put them on a baking sheet, and let them air-dry completely. When the mushrooms are dry, grind them up in a spice grinder and keep the powder in a jar in the freezer.

Chard and Ricotta Tart

The notion of a dessert made with chard may sound bizarre, but it's traditional in the South of France and Italy. Because of the baking powder the pastry will puff as it bakes—the resulting texture is more like a cake than a pie. Serve a small slice of tart with a glass of mint tea to end this meal.

FOR THE DOUGH

2 cups all-purpose flour

1 tablespoon baking powder

½ cup sugar

Pinch of salt

8 tablespoons (1 stick) cold butter,
  cut into small pieces

1 egg, beaten with 1 tablespoon
  milk

Grated zest of ½ lemon

FOR THE FILLING

1 large bunch chard, trimmed, ribs
  discarded, and cut into ½-inch-
  wide strips (about 4 cups)

1 cup whole-milk ricotta

1 egg

⅓ cup sugar

Grated zest of ½ lemon

¼ teaspoon powdered ginger

¼ teaspoon ground allspice

½ cup golden raisins, soaked in
  warm water until plumped

¼ cup pine nuts

To make the dough, in the bowl of an electric mixer, using the flat beater, mix the dry ingredients on low speed. Add the butter and mix for about 2 minutes more, until crumbly. Add the egg mixture and the lemon zest and mix another minute, or until you can pinch the dough together.

Turn the dough out and form 2 balls, one twice as big as the other. Chill for at least an hour.

To make the filling, bring a large pot of salted water to a boil. Blanch the chard for 1 minute; drain well. Let cool, and squeeze out any liquid.

Preheat the oven to 350°F. In a small bowl, whisk together the ricotta, egg, sugar, lemon zest, and spices.

{CONTINUED}

Dust a pastry cloth with flour and roll out the larger dough ball into a circle 2 inches larger than the diameter of your 9- or 10-inch springform pan. Roll the dough onto the rolling pin, then carefully unroll it over the pan and gently press it into place, so that it comes about 2 inches up the sides of the pan. Expect the dough to be pretty soft; if it tears, just press on a scrap to cover any holes.

Drain the raisins, mix them with the greens, and spread over the dough in the pan. Pour the ricotta mixture over the greens and smooth out. Sprinkle the pine nuts over the ricotta.

To make the lattice top, roll out the second piece of dough into a ⅛-inch-thick rectangle. Cut the dough into ¾-inch-wide strips. Fashion a lattice top by alternating crosswise and lengthwise strips. Leave a gap of ¾ inch between strips running in the same direction.

Fold the edges of the bottom crust over the ends of the lattice strips. Bake for 40 to 50 minutes, until the crust is golden.

Cool on a rack before serving.

The Trouble with Ham

Hors d'Oeuvres Variés: Roasted Beet Salad,
   Julienned Carrot Salad, and Leeks Vinaigrette
Petit Salé with Braised Cabbage
Quince Slices (and Beyond)
Walnuts and a Few Cheeses

It's a sad fact of modern life that ham isn't what it used to be, even in some extremely ham-centric cultures. Which is not to say that good ham can't be had—it has just become more of a rarity than a given, at least in North America.

There used to be real ham, real pork in the United States. How did we get from there to canned ham, honey-cooked spiral-cut ham, and Spam? How did we further descend to today's ubiquitous plastic-wrapped, bright pink "cured pork-product, water added"? Most factory-produced cured pork products today taste only of salt and added "natural flavors" and have very little resemblance to their artisanal-made ancestors. More's the pity! Factory farming has robbed a precious foodstuff of its very identity.

There is good news, however. Some small-scale American farms are now producing real pork again, and there is increasing interest among a new generation of cooks in the old preserving methods. So we are sure to see some real ham again in the near future.

In France most butcher shops sell *petit salé,* sometimes called *demi-sel.* This salt-cured pork is rather like a mild cured unsmoked ham, not as salty as our frontier-style salt pork. *Petit salé* was originally designed to preserve pork before the days of refrigeration. As with other forms of cured meat, its unique flavor is still in demand. In France, every part of the pig, from the snout to the tail, goes into the brine bucket. A cook there can buy any of the parts: belly, hock, trotter, ear, loin, shoulder.

When I'm in Paris, it's easy to buy a piece of *petit salé* and bring it home to throw into a pot of lentils. Back in the States, I make my own by mixing up a simple brine in which to submerge a piece of good pork. It's ready in a few days and keeps a week in the fridge. Simmered gently for an hour with a few aromatic vegetables, *petit salé* makes a wonderful meal, accompanied by braised cabbage or sauerkraut, or with wilted greens. You can also cut *petit salé* into lardons to use like bacon in a pot of beans. As a bonus, the resulting delicious broth can be used to make soup.

Hors d'Oeuvres Variés: Roasted Beet Salad, Julienned Carrot Salad, and Leeks Vinaigrette

In a Parisian brasserie, the presentation of simple humble vegetables dressed with vinaigrette is raised to a fine art. The array of a dozen earthenware bowls that greets you as you enter, each with its freshly made vegetable salad, is a purely French thing. I am always shocked by both their ordinariness and their deliciousness.

Thanks to our farmers' markets, we too can find the tastiest vegetables in season. It's all about enjoying each vegetable in its own right: roasted beets, sliced carrots, lovely leeks. Any one of these salads can be a wonderful first course on its own, but man! The sight of them together, so bright, so glistening—piled on one platter or on individual plates—is just too good to miss.

Roasted Beet Salad

Roast your beets the morning of the dinner, or even a day or two before.

6 medium beets
Salt and pepper
1 tablespoon red wine vinegar,
   or more to taste

1 tablespoon sherry vinegar,
   or more to taste
2 teaspoons grated orange zest
½ teaspoon fennel seeds, crushed
¼ cup olive oil

Preheat the oven to 350°F. Wash the beets and put them, unpeeled, in a roasting pan with about an inch of water. Bake, covered, for an hour, or until they are easily pierced with a fork. Slip off the skins while the beets are still warm. (Roasted beets will keep for 2 or 3 days in the refrigerator.)

Dice, slice, or wedge the beets. Put them in a mixing bowl, season with salt and pepper, add the vinegars, and toss well. Add the rest of the seasonings and the oil.

{CONTINUED}

Set aside for a few moments, then taste and reseason as needed. Beets need vinegar, and often after they're dressed, they'll need a bit more.

Transfer the beets to a serving platter and serve at room temperature.

Julienned Carrot Salad

6 large carrots
Salt and pepper
Juice of ½ lemon
1 teaspoon white wine vinegar
Pinch of cayenne

1 garlic clove, smashed to a paste
    with a little salt
3 tablespoons olive oil
2 teaspoons snipped chives
2 teaspoons chopped tarragon

Wash and peel the carrots. Cut them into 2-inch lengths. You want to make short thin strips about the width of thick spaghetti. This you can accomplish with the julienne blade of a food processor, with a mandoline, or with a nice sharp knife.

Put the julienned carrots in a mixing bowl. Season with salt and pepper, add the lemon juice and vinegar, and toss well. Add the cayenne, garlic, and oil. Mix gently but thoroughly. Let sit for about 10 minutes, then check for seasoning.

Transfer to a serving platter. Just before serving, sprinkle with the chives and tarragon.

Leeks Vinaigrette

12 leeks, about ¾ inch in diameter

Salt and pepper

3 tablespoons red wine vinegar

1 small garlic clove, smashed to a
paste with a little salt

1 tablespoon Dijon mustard

¼ cup olive oil

2 teaspoons chopped capers for
garnish (optional)

Wash the leeks. Trim the roots just to the base of the leek, peel off the 2 or 3 outer layers of each leek, and then trim the green tops, leaving a little green on the end. Make a lengthwise slit halfway down each leek and soak the leeks in a large bowl of lukewarm water. Agitate them to remove any sand or grit, lift the leeks from the bowl, and rinse again.

Bring a large pot of well-salted water to a boil. Put in the leeks and simmer briskly until tender, about 10 minutes. Most people either overcook (too mushy) or undercook (too crunchy) leeks. Badly cooked leeks are a terrible waste. To test for doneness, fish out a leek and lay it out on a cutting board. Press it at the thick end with your thumb—there should be a little resistance, but the leek should be soft.

Remove all the leeks from the pot, drain on towels, and then put them in one layer on a platter. Season them lightly with salt and pepper.

In a small bowl, whisk the vinegar, garlic, and mustard, then whisk in the olive oil. The sauce should be slightly thickened. Spoon the vinaigrette over the leeks and let them marinate at room temperature for an hour.

Just before serving, sprinkle with a few chopped capers, if you like.

Petit Salé with Braised Cabbage

Making *petit salé* is essentially like making a mild cured ham: it's a very simple process, but you must begin it 5 days ahead. If you wish, make the cabbage earlier in the day and reheat. SERVES 4 TO 6

FOR THE BRINE

8 cups water

½ cup salt

1 teaspoon black peppercorns

3 or 4 allspice berries

2 bay leaves

1 large sprig fresh thyme or
   1 teaspoon dried thyme

A few whole cloves

1 scant teaspoon curing salt
   (see Note)

2 pounds fresh pork belly,
   skin on

2 pounds fresh pork shanks

FOR THE BROTH

1 onion

1 celery stalk

1 carrot, peeled

Several garlic cloves

A few thyme sprigs

1 bay leaf

2 or 3 whole cloves

A few black peppercorns

Braised Cabbage (recipe follows),
   steaming hot

2 pounds small potatoes, peeled

Chopped parsley for garnish

2 tablespoons freshly grated
   horseradish

¼ cup Dijon mustard

To brine the pork, whisk together all the brine ingredients in a stainless steel or glass bowl or other nonreactive container large enough to hold the meats and brine. Slice the pork belly into 4 or 5 thick pieces. Add all the meat to the brine, and put a plate on top to keep the meat submerged. Cover and refrigerate for 5 days, or up to a week.

To cook the pork, drain the meat and discard the brine. Put the meat in a heavy-bottomed pot and cover with water. Add all the broth ingredients and bring to a boil, then reduce the heat and simmer gently for at least an hour, until the belly is tender and the shank meat is almost falling from the bone. If the belly seems done sooner, take it out and continue cooking the shanks until they're done. Set aside 1 cup of broth in which to braise the cabbage (see below) and reserve the rest for another use, such as in bean or lentil soup.

While the meat is cooking, braise the cabbage. Boil the potatoes in a pot of lightly salted water for 10 to 15 minutes, until tender. Drain and keep warm.

To serve, pile the braised cabbage on a big, deep platter and put the ham shanks on top. Cut the belly into smaller pieces, if you like, and add to the platter. Sprinkle plenty of chopped parsley over the pork. Mix the horseradish and mustard and serve along with the boiled potatoes.

{NOTE ON} CURING SALT

Curing salt, a kind of nitrate also known as *sel rose*, is available online from sausage-making supply companies. Alternatively, you can buy a little from your butcher. You need only a tiny amount for use in brines or ham-making.

Braised Cabbage

I prefer to use a hard green cabbage sometimes called Dutch, but red cabbage is good here too. If you like softer-leaved cabbages such as Savoy or Napa, the cooking time will be much shorter.

2 large onions	1 teaspoon caraway seeds
1 large firm green cabbage	A good pinch of cayenne
2 tablespoons butter	2 tart apples, peeled, cored,
Salt and pepper	and chunked
2 tablespoons sugar	1 cup pork broth (from above)
2 to 3 tablespoons cider vinegar	A small bunch of parsley,
or red wine vinegar	leaves chopped

Slice the onions into half moons, about ⅛ inch thick. Slice the cabbage into ½-inch-wide ribbons.

In a large heavy-bottomed pot, melt the butter. Add the sliced onions, season with salt and pepper, and cook over medium heat until softened, about 5 minutes. Add the sugar, vinegar, caraway seeds, and cayenne, then add the apples and stir gently for a few minutes.

Add the cabbage a handful at a time, salting it lightly as you go. Add the pork broth, raise the heat, put the lid on the pot, and bring to a simmer. Reduce the heat to low and let the cabbage cook, stirring regularly, for about 30 minutes, until quite tender. Sprinkle with the parsley before serving.

QUINCES

The quince is an ancient relative of the apple and looks like a giant apple, yellow-green and fuzzy, with gray-green leaves. Quinces are incredibly aromatic; a basket of freshly picked fruit will perfume the whole house. The tree in blossom is a sight to behold: the flower is bright pink. And when the fruits ripen in late September, the trees are heavy with it, bowed almost to the ground, or propped up with sticks.

Quinces must be cooked to be edible; otherwise, they are far too astringent. Common uses are quince jelly—easy to make, since quinces are full of natural pectin—but quinces are good too as an addition to apples in a pie. The fruit may be best known as quince paste: *membrillo* in Spain, and *pâte de coing* in France. Quince paste can be sliced for a little dessert, or paired with cheese, usually an aged sheep's-milk. In Sicily, the paste is called *cotognata* and made from an old quince varietal. In Mexico, fruit paste made with quince, guava, and other fruits is called *ate.* Argentina loves *membrillo* too, almost as much as she loves dulce de leche.

Quince Slices (and Beyond)

This recipe is a three-stage journey from raw quince to *membrillo*. In the first stage, you make a fine dessert of sliced quinces poached in a sugar syrup, and as a side benefit, you get a jar of quince-flavored syrup. Then the slices can become quince marmalade, and finally be cooked down to *membrillo*.

6 medium quinces   4 cups water
6 cups sugar

Raw quinces are a little difficult to peel. What I do is quarter the quinces, peel each quarter and remove the core with a paring knife, and then slice each peeled quarter lengthwise into thirds. Discard the peels, but save the cores. Tie them in a piece of cheesecloth to add pectin to the syrup.

In a heavy-bottomed nonreactive pot (enameled or stainless steel), heat the sugar with the water, stirring to dissolve the sugar. Add the quince slices and cores, and simmer gently, stirring occasionally, for 30 to 40 minutes, or until the quince slices are tender. Discard the cores. Cool the quince slices in the syrup.

Quince slices in syrup make a delicious dessert—so intense, you need only 2 or 3 slices per serving. And such a lovely rose color. Quince syrup with yogurt is a satanically good combination.

Stop here, or continue the journey to quince marmalade or quince paste.

To make marmalade, ladle off some of the syrup, so the quinces are barely covered in liquid. Return the pot to the stove and bring to a boil over medium-high heat, then reduce the heat and simmer briskly for 30 minutes, stirring frequently. Basically, you're cooking away the water and thickening the jam. By this point, the fruit should be very soft, with little liquid remaining. Remove the pan from the stove.

{CONTINUED}

Mash the quinces with a potato masher, but leave them rather chunky. Check the consistency. If the marmalade seems too thin, put it back on the stove for a few minutes, but remember it will thicken upon cooling. Spoon the marmalade into a jar and store in the refrigerator.

To make *membrillo,* the last step on the quince's journey, grind up the marmalade in a food processor or a meat grinder. Depending upon the thickness, you might have to cook it a little more. Take a spoonful, spread it on a plate, and put the plate in the refrigerator for an hour. If it is nicely jelled at this point, the quince mixture is ready to pour into a terrine or other mold that has been oiled with olive oil or lined with plastic wrap. Chill the mold for 24 hours.

To serve, unmold the *membrillo* and cut into thin slices.

Walnuts and a Few Cheeses

Fall is a good time to look for new-crop walnuts and cheeses at your local farmers' market. Wherever you are in the States, there are good artisanal cheese makers, and a sampling of their local offerings can make an excellent cheese course.

The rule of thumb for a balanced cheese plate is to have a range of textures, from soft to semi-hard to firm, and a variety of cheeses, from goat's, sheep's, and cow's milk, as well. But it's sometimes more interesting to taste three kinds of goat's-milk cheese, or three kinds of cow's-milk. Three cheeses are plenty.

Winter Menus

menu sixteen

COOKING FOR TOMORROW TODAY

Terrine of Pork and Duck Liver

Duck Confit in the Oven with Crispy Panfried Potatoes

Celery, Radish, and Watercress Salad with Walnut Oil

An Honest Loaf

Spiced Pears in Red Wine

menu seventeen

DEAD-OF-WINTER DINNER FROM THE SUPERMARKET

Romaine Hearts with Shaved Parmigiano and Lemon Dressing

Panfried Steak with Steak Sauce

Classic Potato Gratin

Broiled Pineapple with Rum

menu eighteen

SWEET STEW

Savory Baked Eggs in Filo

Fragrant Lamb with Prunes and Almonds

Blood Oranges and Pomegranates with Orange Flower Water

menu nineteen

OF BUCKWHEAT AND MUSSELS

Buckwheat Galettes with Ham and Cheese

Mâche Salad

Mussels Marinière, Brittany-Style

Apple Compote

Butter Cookies

menu twenty

BRING BACK TONGUE

Greens on Toast

Bollito Misto of Tongue and Brisket with Two Sauces

Walnut and Pine Nut Drops

Cooking for Tomorrow Today

Terrine of Pork and Duck Liver
Duck Confit in the Oven with Crispy Panfried Potatoes
Celery, Radish, and Watercress Salad with Walnut Oil
An Honest Loaf
Spiced Pears in Red Wine

The 30-minute meal ain't all it's cracked up to be. Slinging dinner on the table may feed us, but such hurried gestures often bypass the pleasure that real cooking offers. Spending a day in the kitchen can be amazingly rewarding—the reward is the mellowness of flavor and texture that results when certain dishes are given the luxury of improving over time.

A terrine, for example, needs a few days for the flavors to develop and is better even a week later. Duck confit is the ultimate make-ahead dish; a side benefit is that the flavor improves as you wait for the day when it becomes a crispy, delicious thing. Confits, pâtés, and sausages were devised as a way to preserve meat, but they become more delectable in the process. Likewise, everything about baking bread is better the next day. The dough always improves after a night in the refrigerator—the flavor as well as the texture. And pears poached in red wine are so much better after a night's rest deepens their color and flavor.

Winter weather frequently keeps us indoors. Why not pass the time cooking up a little something for a future meal or two?

Terrine of Pork and Duck Liver

Rustic terrines and pâtés have been out of fashion for so long that I think the whole art form is due for re-examination.

This terrine is solid, the kind small purveyors bring to market in Paris. Most country-style terrines are rustic looking and meat-loaf-colored. For a rosier terrine, add a small amount of curing salt.

2 pounds boneless pork shoulder
½ pound duck or chicken livers
Salt
½ teaspoon black peppercorns
4 allspice berries
4 whole cloves
¼ teaspoon coriander seeds
4 garlic cloves
Pinch of cayenne
¼ cup dry white wine

1 tablespoon Cognac or other brandy
Scant ½ teaspoon curing salt (optional)
1 teaspoon finely chopped thyme
1 teaspoon finely chopped sage
Pickled Onions (recipe follows)
Cornichons
Dijon mustard

Make sure to have the butcher chop the pork on the largest holes of his meat grinder. Or, you can hand-chop the meat, cutting it into ⅛-inch dice with a big sharp knife or a cleaver. Transfer the chopped meat to a large bowl.

Trim the livers. Put them in a blender or a food processor and puree. Pour over the chopped pork in the bowl. Add 2 teaspoons salt and mix well with your hands. Refrigerate the meat until it's quite cold.

In a mortar or spice grinder, powder the peppercorns, allspice, cloves, and coriander seeds.

Pound the garlic in a mortar with a little salt. Stir in the powdered spices, cayenne, white wine, Cognac, curing salt, if using, thyme, and sage.

Knead the spice mixture into the meat in the bowl with your hands. Cover and refrigerate to let the flavors meld for at least a couple of hours, or as long as overnight. It will smell delicious already.

Make a small skinny patty of the meat mixture and fry it to taste the seasoning. It should be highly seasoned. This is your last chance to make adjustments!

When you're ready to bake the terrine, preheat the oven to 375°F. Put the meat mixture in an 8-inch loaf pan or an earthenware baking dish. Cover the terrine tightly with foil.

Put the pan on a baking sheet, and then into the oven. Bake for 45 minutes, then remove the foil and bake for another 15 minutes, or until the terrine is nicely browned. The meat will look like it's floating in liquid, and that's a good thing. These juices will eventually surround the terrine with a tasty jelly. Check the temperature of the terrine with an instant-read thermometer. The center of the loaf should read 150°F. When it's done, carefully remove the terrine from the oven, making sure not to spill the hot juices, and let it cool to room temperature.

Wrap the terrine well with plastic wrap and refrigerate for at least a day or two. For this kind of rustic pâté, I don't find it necessary to weight the terrine as is classically done.

To serve the terrine, run a knife around the edges and slice it in the pan, or invert it onto a cutting board and slice it at the table. Serve with the pickled onions, cornichons, and Dijon mustard.

{VARIATION} ANOTHER WAY TO BAKE A TERRINE

Perhaps you don't have a loaf pan or terrine. You can form the meat into a long sausage shape, about 3 inches in diameter by 12 inches. Wrap the meat in pastry (you can use the dough in the recipe on pages 102–3).

Put the sausage on a baking sheet and bake for about 45 minutes at 375°F. Store the sausage in the refrigerator for a day or two before slicing.

To serve, cut it into thick slices. Its looks are reminiscent of a fat French garlic sausage.

Pickled Onions

Make these easy pickles the day before you serve the terrine.

4 small white onions,
   cut into ¼-inch rings
2 cups water
1 tablespoon salt
2 teaspoons turmeric
3 whole cloves

2 allspice berries
½ cup white wine vinegar
1 thyme sprig
1 bay leaf
¼ cup sugar

Put the onions in a glass or stainless steel bowl. Bring the water to a boil in a small saucepan, then add all the other ingredients and simmer for 5 minutes.

Pour the boiling brine over the onions. Let cool to room temperature, then transfer the onions to a jar. (They will keep for a month, refrigerated.)

Duck Confit in the Oven with Crispy Panfried Potatoes

The process of making confit of anything (*confit* means preserve, as in confiture of fruits, which are jams) involves simmering seasoned meats in fat and then preserving them in their cooking fat. In the olden days, these meats were stored in a cool cellar, where the layer of fat essentially hermetically sealed the meat against bacteria.

A typical French farmhouse would put up duck or goose confit, various braised parts of the pig, and even sausages in this manner. There's an oft-repeated story of a French farmwife embarrassed because she has nothing to serve an unexpected visitor but some duck confit—a treat any of us would be delighted by.

Nobody except that farm cook would have enough duck fat on hand to make this dish, so I've developed a method to get the same deep flavor of duck confit without requiring a gallon of duck fat to do it. Besides, since we store the results in a refrigerator these days, we do not need all that fat. I prefer Pekin, or Long Island, to Muscovy duck legs because I find that the meat is more tender.

Still and all, making this confit is a two-day process, because you must let the seasoned duck legs stand overnight, then cook the duck for a couple of hours the next day. And the legs should mellow in the fridge for a day or two after that before serving them. SERVES 4 TO 6

8 duck legs, preferably Pekin or
   Long Island
Salt and pepper
4 garlic cloves, roughly chopped
1 tablespoon fresh thyme, roughly
   chopped, or crumbled dried thyme

1 cup rendered duck fat
   (see page 228)
Crispy Panfried Potatoes
   (page 229)

Trim the duck legs of excess skin and fat, reserving the trimmings for rendering, and lay them out on a baking sheet. Season well with salt and pepper on both sides. Sprinkle the chopped garlic and thyme over the legs and massage into the meat. Put the duck legs in a covered container and refrigerate overnight.

The next day, bring the duck legs to room temperature. Preheat the oven to 350°F. Rinse the garlic and thyme from the duck legs with cool water and pat them dry.

Heat the rendered duck fat in a small pan. Lay the duck legs in one layer in a deep baking dish, skin side down. Pour the duck fat over the legs and add 2 cups of water. Cover the pan tightly with foil and bake for 1½ hours, or until the meat is quite tender at the bone when probed with the

tip of a paring knife. The meat should not have browned at all; you'll brown it just before serving. Carefully remove the pan from the oven and let cool.

Transfer the cooled duck legs to a covered container, and pour the strained cooking liquid over them. Put in the refrigerator to mellow for a day or two.

To cook the duck legs, bring them to room temperature and preheat the oven to 375°F. Leaving a bit of fat clinging to each leg, carefully scrape most of the fat off and reserve it for frying the potatoes (save any tasty duck jelly separately from the fat). Put the duck legs skin side up in one layer in a low roasting pan, and put the pan in the oven.

Roast the legs for about 30 minutes, basting occasionally, until the skin is crisp and brown. Remove the duck from the oven, blot the legs with paper towels, and put them on a platter with a pile of the panfried potatoes.

A RENDERING LESSON

Rendering is simply the process of extracting fat through slow simmering. Duck fat is a wonderful, tasty fat to cook in, still used extensively in the southwest of France, the duck capital of the world. Although you can buy duck fat already rendered, it's costly. But it is not hard to make and is satisfying to do.

The trimmings from the 8 legs in the duck confit recipe will yield about a cup of rendered fat. Put the saved trimmings in a small pan, add a cup of water, and simmer gently for 30 to 40 minutes. Strain the liquid and cool it, then store the duck fat in a glass jar in the refrigerator. Note: Rendered duck fat keeps for months. There will be a small amount of flavorful jelly at the bottom of the jar, which you'll want to save for sauces or soups. The rest of the jar contains the delicious fat you'll use to finish cooking the duck legs and make the potatoes crispy.

Crispy Panfried Potatoes

Use any kind of baking potato here. Common russets are fine, but I prefer large yellow-fleshed potatoes like Yukon Gold or Bintje. Just don't use waxy boiling potatoes, because they won't get crisp. If you don't have duck fat, use olive oil, clarified butter, or good-quality lard. Duck fat makes the tastiest crispy potatoes.

2 to 3 pounds baking potatoes, peeled and cut into 1-inch cubes

Duck fat for frying (see A Rendering Lesson, opposite)

2 garlic cloves, mashed to a paste with a little salt

2 tablespoons chopped parsley

Salt and pepper

Boil the potatoes in a large pot of salted water for 10 minutes, or until cooked through but still firm. Drain the potatoes, spread them on a baking sheet, and allow them to cool to room temperature. (You can do this well ahead of time, then brown the potatoes while the duck is cooking.)

Heat a large cast-iron skillet over medium-high heat and add ½ inch of duck fat. When the fat is hot, carefully add the potatoes to the pan in one layer. Try to resist touching them until they begin to brown and loosen from the pan. Gently turn them with a slotted spoon or spatula and let them cook for another 10 minutes, or until they're nicely browned on all sides.

Lift the potatoes from the fat and blot them on paper towels. Put the potatoes in a wide mixing bowl, add the garlic and parsley, season well with salt and pepper, and toss well. Serve on the same platter with duck confit or in a warmed serving vessel.

Celery, Radish, and Watercress Salad with Walnut Oil

In the winter, you crave bright, fresh greens alongside all these long slow-cooked dishes to add a little zip to the meal.

2 small bunches watercress	Salt and pepper
1 small shallot, finely diced	5 to 6 tablespoons walnut oil
1 tablespoon red wine vinegar	1 celery heart, thinly sliced
1 tablespoon sherry vinegar	8 radishes, slivered

Wash the watercress well. This is easier to do if you keep the bunches intact. Swish each one in a large bowl of water, then drain it, still in a bunch, upside down in a colander. Shake off the excess water. Carefully cut the leafy tops away from the stems and roll them in a kitchen towel. Refrigerate until ready to serve.

To make the vinaigrette, put the shallot in a small bowl and add the vinegars, with a pinch of salt. Grind in a little pepper, whisk in the walnut oil, taste, and correct the seasonings.

To serve, put the celery and radishes in a salad bowl. Season with salt and pepper, then add the vinaigrette and toss. Add the watercress sprigs, toss lightly, and serve immediately.

An Honest Loaf

Making bread is squarely in the spirit of good things well worth the wait. There is such a craze these days for all kinds of shortcuts like bread machines, or for making fast-rising, instant loaves. Obviously, I think they miss the whole point of making bread. I like my hands in the dough. I like waiting for the dough to rise, knowing it needs time to mature and that a slow, cool rise is the best way to get good bread.

For this loaf, you stir up a starter and let it stand for a while. Then you mix the dough and let it rest overnight in the refrigerator. The next day, you knead the dough, form the loaf, and allow it to rise slowly in a floured basket for several hours.

After it rises, you invert the loaf onto a baking sheet and shove it into a hot oven: the baking sheet and the heat of the oven ensure a beautiful crust. Once it's baked, try to resist nibbling until the loaf has cooled completely. In fact, if you can wait, a loaf like this is even better the following day. This bread is not like a baguette that's better within a few hours of baking; it is a keeping loaf, and it will provide several days of sandwiches and toast.

1 tablespoon active dry yeast
2 cups lukewarm water
2 cups unbleached bread flour
½ cup whole wheat flour

½ cup semolina, plus extra for
   dusting
2 teaspoons salt

Put the yeast and water in a large mixing bowl. Stir in 1 cup of the bread flour to make a thick batter. The mixture should begin to bubble almost immediately, signifying that the yeast is doing its job (basically, we just fed the yeast a little snack). Leave the mixture at room temperature for about an hour, until it's quite frothy and has risen in the bowl.

{CONTINUED}

Add the white flour, whole wheat flour, semolina, and salt to the starter and stir well. When the dough is gathered but still shaggy, turn it out onto a lightly floured counter and knead it for just a couple of minutes, dusting it lightly with flour if necessary; the dough should remain a little sticky.

Put the dough in a mixing bowl, cover with plastic wrap, and refrigerate overnight. The dough will rise a bit in the bowl.

The next day, remove the dough from the bowl and punch it down to get the air out. Knead the dough again for a few minutes, and form it into a smooth ball.

Select a basket or bowl large enough to contain the dough when it doubles in size: if you happen to have a French-linen-lined dough-rising basket, by all means use that; otherwise, line a low wide bowl with a linen napkin and dust it heavily with white flour before you add the dough. Set the dough ball into the basket or bowl, dust the top with semolina, and cover loosely with plastic wrap. Let the dough rise at cool room temperature for 2 to 3 hours, or until doubled in size. The longer and cooler the rise, the better the texture of the bread will be.

Preheat the oven to 450°F—make sure it's thoroughly preheated, so you'll be putting the bread into a very hot oven. Sprinkle a baking sheet with semolina. Place the dough onto the baking sheet by carefully inverting the basket or bowl over the sheet; remove the basket (or napkin). The top of the dough will have a light coating of flour. Sprinkle on a bit more.

With a sharp, thin knife or razor blade, quickly slash a large X in the top of the dough, about ½ inch deep. Immediately put the pan in the oven. Bake for 15 minutes. The loaf will puff dramatically and the crust will have begun to form.

Turn down the oven to 400°F and bake for 45 minutes more, or until the bread is dark and crusty. Remove the bread from the oven and put it on a cooling rack. As the bread cools, you'll hear it making crackling sounds. That is the sound of an honest loaf.

BAKING BREAD

Making a loaf of bread can be seen as the quintessential act of cooking. To gather seeds, crush them, mix them with water to form a cake, and bake the cake on a hot stone—this is the work of man and no other. I began cooking in earnest after I taught myself to bake a loaf of bread from a recipe in *The New York Times.* I was seventeen. The recipe was for Cuban bread, a crusty white loaf: yeast, water, flour, salt, maybe a pinch of sugar. Cornmeal on the baking sheet, and a shallow pan of water in the bottom of the oven for steam. The kneaded loaf was allowed to rise, then slashed and baked. I was mesmerized by the aroma.

I began baking more complex loaves (this was innocence, as I know now the best loaves are the plainest). I fell for hand-ground wheat berries to make a coarse whole wheat bread; I combined whole wheat pastry flour, sunflower seeds, coconut, and walnuts for the then-popular hippie loaf. I mastered challah and rye bread. And after that it was just a short jump to pies, and pizzas, and focaccia. I even worked for a time as a professional baker, learning to make croissants, puff pastry, brioche, and the like, but I still prefer more rustic breads.

Although today there are more and more good bakeries, it's nonetheless extremely satisfying to bake a loaf of bread.

Spiced Pears in Red Wine

Poached pears in red wine is a classic French dessert. It's the overnight bath that stains the pears a deep, rich red and infuses them with flavor. When this dessert is overspiced, it tastes like bad mulled wine. I prefer it on the subtle side.

8 slightly underripe small Comice or Anjou pears	1 bay leaf
1 (750-ml) bottle medium-bodied red wine, such as Côtes du Rhone	1 teaspoon fennel seeds
	2 whole cloves
1½ cups sugar	A wide strip each of lemon and orange peel

Peel the pears top to bottom with a sharp vegetable peeler, leaving them whole, with stems attached and the core intact.

Put the pears in a large wide nonreactive pot (enameled or stainless steel) in one layer. Stir the wine and sugar together in a bowl to dissolve the sugar, pour over the pears, and add the aromatics. Cover and bring to a boil, then reduce the heat to a gentle simmer. Poach the pears for about 30 minutes or until a skewer inserted encounters no resistance. Remove from the heat and let cool, in the poaching liquid, overnight.

The next day, with a slotted spoon, transfer the pears to a platter. Heat the poaching liquid over high and boil down until it is reduced by half. Strain this syrup into a bowl and let cool.

Use a paring knife to cut a small slice off the bottom of each pear, allowing them to stand up straight. Stand the pears in a deep rectangular glass or plastic container large enough to contain them in one layer.

Pour the cooled syrup over the pears. Refrigerate for up to several days. Serve chilled, putting each pear in a soup plate and spooning over a little syrup.

Dead-of-Winter Dinner from the Supermarket

Romaine Hearts with Shaved Parmigiano and Lemon Dressing
Panfried Steak with Steak Sauce
Classic Potato Gratin
Broiled Pineapple with Rum

It is true, the supermarket is not the first place I head when I set out to go food shopping. I was raised on supermarket food and a trip there as a child always seemed fun, but as I grew older, I discovered so many more interesting places to find good ingredients. Farmers' markets and farm stands, of course, but I also found I was happier in a Latino market or wandering through Chinatown. Still, for many people, the supermarket is the only choice.

It has to be said that what is available in supermarkets today is a heck of a lot better than what you could find even ten years ago. But a supermarket crawl in January in New York City left me with strong impressions: no matter the progress, the primary concern of these places is not the selling of good food. Theirs is the well-stocked shelf laden with the packaged and the processed—with baking mixes and instant soups and breakfast cereals and snack foods. A savvy shopper can, and should, try not to be seduced by the processed stuff, and instead seek out only what seems like real food.

There were some encouraging signs, however. I noted a number of supermarkets where a good butcher or fish counter can be found (although I still don't know many with good prepared deli food, or with a bakery that produces much more than bread that smells good). I was also pleased with the proliferation of naturally raised beef; you pay a bit more, but you get your money's worth in flavor and healthy planetness. I was reminded that fresh turkey and fresh turkey parts are widely available. I was encouraged by the increased presence of better chickens and healthier eggs. In produce-land, I still have a strong antipathy for premixed lettuce in cellophane bags. Carefully packaged arugula, though, seems to be surviving the trip, and hearts of organic romaine lettuce abound, for an easy and satisfying salad.

As I wandered the aisles, the big shock was discovering row upon row of bottled sauces and dressings. Perusing the ingredients lists with a magnifying glass, I discovered that what lurked in the fine print was most often one dread ingredient: high-fructose corn syrup. And a lot of it. I always knew that there were ready-made salad dressings for people who are daunted by the idea of mixing a little oil and vinegar, but I was astounded by the array (and the cost!) of cooking sauces, barbecue sauces, steak sauces, glazes, and marinades—many of which had a famous person's picture on the label. Wonder what Ernest Hemingway would think about his namesake marinades in the flavors of Key West, Kenya, and Idaho Mesquite. The companies that make all these prepared sauces prey on our fear of cooking, and on the notion that we somehow inherently believe we do not have time to cook.

This mad array of expensive, unhealthy, and inauthentic bottles made me want to do two things: to work out an easy steak sauce for the common man, and to scout the aisles for more supermarket food that I could happily cook.

Romaine Hearts with Shaved Parmigiano and Lemon Dressing

I'm usually desperate for salad in winter, and clearly there's not much lettuce growing anywhere nearby. But here you must bend the rules for seasonal eating, because good salad is both a luxury and a necessity. The one thing you can count on in the supermarket is the ubiquity of organic romaine hearts, even though they're packaged like rolls of paper towels, and sometimes you have to reach to the back of the shelf for the most recently shipped. I usually buy more than I need so that I can pare back a few of the outer leaves of each head to reveal the tender, pale hearts within. Those are the leaves to use.

This is a flavor combination I always crave: romaine, lemon, and Parmigiano. I never tire of this salad. It's easy, versatile, and, though it can be made at any time of the year, is especially welcome in the dead of winter.

4 romaine hearts

3 tablespoons fresh lemon juice

1 teaspoon Dijon mustard

1 garlic clove, smashed to a paste
   with a little salt

¼ cup olive oil

Salt and pepper

A chunk of Parmigiano
   for shaving

First prepare the romaine hearts: Cut off the bottoms, and discard a few of the outer leaves of each head. Gently separate the inner leaves and refresh in a deep basin of cold water for just a minute. Drain well, wrap in kitchen towels, and refrigerate. The whole idea is that they should look fresh and crisp.

Now make the dressing: In a small bowl, stir together the lemon juice, mustard, and garlic. Whisk in the olive oil and season well with salt and pepper. Taste and correct the seasoning if necessary; the dressing should be rather tart.

{CONTINUED}

Put the leaves in a large salad bowl. Sprinkle lightly with salt, pour the dressing over the lettuce, and gently coat the leaves, tossing with your hands. With a vegetable peeler, shave large curls of Parmigiano over the salad.

{VARIATION} WITH BLUE CHEESE
Replace the Parmigiano with rough shards of Roquefort or other blue cheese. Although supermarkets carry precrumbled blue cheeses, why pay extra for something inferior? For best results, crumble your own!

{VARIATION} WITH ANCHOVY DRESSING
Rinse 3 anchovy fillets in a bowl of warm water, then soak in ¼ cup milk for 15 minutes to mellow. Remove the anchovies from the milk and blot on paper towels. Mash 2 garlic cloves with the anchovies in a mortar. Add a little salt to help create a paste. Add a little finely chopped lemon zest, the juice of half a lemon, and a splash of champagne vinegar. Stir in 2 teaspoons Dijon mustard and, gradually, ⅓ cup olive oil, until you have a thickish vinaigrette. Check the seasoning, and correct with lemon juice, salt, and/or freshly ground black pepper.

Panfried Steak with Steak Sauce

Why go out for a steak dinner with all the trimmings? All you need is a good piece of meat. Obviously, the better the supermarket, the better the meat department is likely to be, but you can find a good butcher in the most surprising places. I tend to trust those markets where they're cutting the meat before my eyes. If you can find a butcher, ask him to cut you some nice steaks for panfrying. A well-marbled rib eye makes a beautiful if somewhat pricey steak, but so do cheaper cuts like flatiron or hanger steak.

Whichever, I always prefer restrained portions: 5 or 6 ounces per steak is plenty. Buy one steak for each person.

4 to 6 steaks, about 1 inch thick	½ cup Brown Turkey Stock
Salt and pepper	(recipe follows) or beef broth
4 garlic cloves, thickly sliced	2 tablespoons butter
Olive oil	2 tablespoons chopped parsley

Season the steaks generously on both sides with salt and coarsely ground pepper. Scatter the garlic over the steaks, then drizzle over a little olive oil and rub it into the steaks. Set aside at cool room temperature for an hour or so. (Or cover and refrigerate, and return to room temperature in a few hours.)

You'll need two skillets, preferably cast-iron, to cook the steaks. Heat the pans until they're really hot. Remove the garlic slices from the steaks and discard. When the pans are good and hot, lay 3 steaks in each pan and let them sizzle. Do not touch them, do not move them. After 3 minutes, inspect the cooked side to see if it's beautifully seared and browned, and when it is, turn each steak over. Cook on the second side just until the juices appear on the surface, about 2 minutes more. Remove the steaks to a warm platter. Leave the pans on the stove, but turn off the heat.

To quickly make the steak sauce, pour ¼ cup stock into each pan, stirring with a wooden spoon to deglaze. Pour all of the deglazed juices into one of the pans, turn up the heat to high, and quickly cook down the sauce to thicken slightly, then stir in the butter and parsley. Turn off the heat, swirl the pan to mix well, and spoon the sauce over the steaks.

{VARIATION} PANFRIED STEAK WITH HERB BUTTER
Instead of a sauce, make a simple herb butter to smear on the steaks: Mix 2 tablespoons finely chopped parsley into 4 tablespoons softened butter and add a small garlic clove, pounded to a paste with a little salt. Spread a teaspoon or so over each finished steak on the platter. You could, of course, use a small shallot, finely diced, instead of the garlic, or another herb, such as tarragon, chives, or rosemary.

Brown Turkey Stock

Turkey's a bird we don't think about much except for the holidays, but supermarkets seem to consider it a staple all year round. Usually I'm not much of a fan of ground turkey (I'd rather have a real burger)—the other parts interest me. The wings and the necks make a beautiful brown stock, the legs can be braised like osso buco, and legs plus wings will make a *dinde au vin,* the turkey version of coq au vin (it's easier to find a turkey than a rooster these days). The breasts can be sliced for turkey scaloppine or roasted (see page 311).

Fresh turkey carcasses, wings, and bony bits can substitute for chicken in making a wonderful broth. You can use this brown stock for a number of things: to make a simple pan sauce (as in the preceding recipe) for steaks or chops, or to enrich soups or braises. MAKES 1 QUART STOCK

1 pound turkey wings and necks	½ cup dry red wine
1 small onion, roughly chopped	6 cups water
1 small carrot, roughly chopped	

Preheat the oven to 400°F. Put all the ingredients except the water in a roasting pan and roast for 30 to 40 minutes, until everything is well and nicely browned. Stir occasionally.

Transfer the contents of the pan to a large saucepan on the stove and add the water. Rinse the roasting pan with a little water to capture any brown bits, and add them to the saucepan. Bring to a boil, then reduce to a simmer. Skim off any rising foam and simmer very gently for 45 minutes to an hour. Strain and refrigerate the stock. The stock should be intensely brown and slightly jelled when cold. It will keep for up to 1 week in the refrigerator, or you can freeze it.

Classic Potato Gratin

A good potato gratin is probably the one thing you can serve at any dinner table that everybody will love. Of all the versions, I prefer this traditional French-style gratin, made simply with potatoes, cream, and butter.

3 pounds baking potatoes
  (use medium russet, Bintje,
  or German Butterball)
Salt and pepper

4 tablespoons butter, plus a little
  more for the baking dish
2½ cups organic heavy cream,
  or as needed

Preheat the oven to 375°F. Peel the potatoes and put them in a bowl of cold water. Smear a baking dish thickly with butter. My favorite gratin dish is a circular pan 14 inches in diameter and 2 inches deep. If you don't have a large dish, make 2 smaller gratins. Just make sure the dish is not too deep.

To assemble the gratin, place a cutting board on the counter between the bowl of potatoes and the baking dish. Using a mandoline, if you have one, slice a few potatoes at a time, as thin as possible. Quickly lay the potato slices in the bottom of the pan, overlapping them to make one layer. Sprinkle lightly with salt and pepper. Slice a few more potatoes and make another layer. Continue in this fashion, seasoning each layer, until all the potatoes are used.

Pour the cream over the potatoes and tilt the pan to distribute it well. With your hands, push down on the top layer to even out the pile. The cream should just barely cover the potatoes. Add a little more if necessary. Dot the surface with the butter, then cover the dish tightly with foil and put it in the oven. Bake for 30 minutes.

Remove the foil and return the pan to the oven for another 30 minutes or so to brown the top of the gratin. Let the gratin rest for 10 minutes before serving. (The gratin can also be cooled and left at room temperature for several hours, and reheated in a moderate oven.)

{GRATIN VARIATIONS}

Obviously, there are many other delicious ways to make a gratin. For a good cheesy version, sprinkle an assertive cheese, such as Swiss Gruyère or Raclette, or even Fontina, between each layer of potatoes. You'll need about 2 cups grated cheese.

There's a Swedish version of the dish called Jansson's Temptation, which calls for anchovies and onions and is excellent for breakfast or lunch. To make a good approximation of Jansson's, mix 1 large onion, sliced thin, with about 12 anchovy fillets, rinsed and roughly chopped, and divide the mixture among the layers. Bake as for the classic gratin.

Broiled Pineapple with Rum

What a luxury to have a ripe pineapple in the middle of winter—and supermarkets often do. The smaller pineapples tend to be the sweetest. A sour, stringy pineapple is a disaster, but a sweet ripe fruit can be a revelation.

Cutting a pineapple is almost like carving a pumpkin. There's a real art to it. Using a serrated knife, cut off the top and bottom of the fruit, then peel away the skin along the curves. Now you must remove the "eyes" that run around the exterior in a spiral. To do this, with a sharp paring knife, cut a grooved channel in the surface, following the eyes. Work around the pineapple in a circular spiral fashion.

Now you can slice the fruit into rounds. Or slice the pineapple into quarters, remove the core, and slice into wedges to serve cool and fresh. Still, there's also something nice about a broiled pineapple. Preheat the broiler. Cut the peeled pineapple into quarters, remove the core, and cut into ½-inch slices. Spread the slices in one layer in a ceramic or glass baking dish, sprinkle lightly with brown sugar, and bake for about 10 minutes, until the pineapple begins to brown a bit. Remove the pineapple from the oven. Heat ¼ cup of rum in a small saucepan and pour the rum over the pineapple slices. Strike a match, carefully light the rum, and flame the fruit. When the flame subsides, serve the pineapple warm from the dish, or at room temperature.

Sweet Stew

Savory Baked Eggs in Filo
Fragrant Lamb with Prunes and Almonds
Blood Oranges and Pomegranates with Orange Flower Water

Over time, I've learned that there are many kinds of cooks. There are people who understand how to roast and those who understand how to grill. There are cooks who love to turn up the heat and sauté in a hot pan and those who are masters at frying. There are the cooks who really, really know how to stew and braise and boil. And while all good cooks have parts of some of these cooks in them, it's well worth cultivating the part of you that yearns to stew.

If I had my way, I would launch a Society for the Protection of Long-Cooked Stews. Its members would braise regularly, cultivating their skill until they feel it innately, instead of being culinary gadflies, forever distracted by the newest recipe or the trendiest ingredient and never perfecting anything well enough to make it theirs. I can't emphasize enough how important the recurring stew theme can be in your kitchen. The satisfying process of nursing a winter braise is a discipline whose one demand is that you slow down and learn to recognize what you're looking for. Every time you make it, you'll discover more about it.

The whole project may take a few days, and that's part of the point. A braise always tastes better the day after it's made. It used to be that people went to the butcher and knew what to look for in braising meat. Besides lamb shanks—which *are* wonderful to slow-cook—you could get meaty neck bones, or a small shoulder of lamb on the bone, or several thick-cut shoulder chops. Beef short ribs or bone-in beef chuck makes wonderful stews, as do meaty beef shanks.

Generally speaking, the forward parts of the animal are best for braising; the rear parts are better for grilling and roasting.

I have always found the Moroccan tagine to be a cozy port in a stormy world. The difference between a tagine and the European meat ragout is the range of ingredients, the depth of color. Tagines offer a kind of opulence. I think of them as polychromatic. Typically it's a knowing mix of sweet and savory—not just of spice, but of fruit too, and buttery onions as fragrant as a Moroccan spice shop.

Savory Baked Eggs in Filo

A savory egg dish is a common first course in Morocco and Tunisia. To make these simple baked eggs, you must first bake the filo pastry cups. You can do this several hours ahead.

6 sheets filo dough

8 tablespoons (1 stick) butter, melted

3 tablespoons olive oil

1 large onion, sliced

Salt and pepper

1 garlic clove, smashed to a paste with a little salt

½ teaspoon cayenne or hot red chile powder

½ teaspoon cumin seeds, toasted and ground

6 large organic eggs

Lemon wedges

Coriander sprigs for garnish

Harissa Oil (recipe follows) (optional)

Preheat the oven to 375°. To make the pastries, lay a 12-inch square sheet of filo flat on the counter. Paint it generously with melted butter and fold it in half. Paint again with butter and fold once more. Invert a 5½-inch bowl over the folded sheet and with a paring knife carefully cut a circle. Gently press the circle of filo into a muffin tin. Repeat with the remaining pastry sheets until you have six little filo cups. Bake for 5 minutes, until just barely golden. Cool. Leave the oven on.

Heat the olive oil in a large skillet over medium heat. Add the onion, season with salt and pepper, and let it brown slightly, then turn down the heat. Cook, stirring occasionally, until the onion is soft, about 5 minutes. Add the garlic, cayenne, and cumin and cook for a minute longer, then transfer the onion mixture to a bowl to cool. Taste and adjust the seasoning: it should be a little kicky.

{CONTINUED}

Spoon a little of the onion filling into each pastry cup. Break an egg into each cup and season with salt and pepper.

Bake for 10 to 15 minutes, until the eggs are set but the yolks are still runny. Serve warm on a platter with lemon wedges, garnished with sprigs of coriander. If you'd like a little extra spice, drizzle with Harissa Oil.

Harissa Oil

Delicious with the Savory Baked Eggs in Filo, harissa oil can be drizzled over any number of things—olives, vegetables, toasted bread, or chicken stew.
MAKES ABOUT 1 CUP

1 tablespoon cumin seeds

1 tablespoon coriander seeds

1 teaspoon caraway seeds

1 teaspoon fennel seeds

3 tablespoons sweet paprika or
   mild ground red chile

1 teaspoon cayenne or other
   powdered hot red chile

1 to 2 garlic cloves, smashed to
   a paste with a little salt

1 teaspoon salt

1 cup olive oil

A few drops of red wine vinegar

Toast all the seeds in a dry pan over medium heat until they are fragrant. Grind the toasted seeds in a mortar or spice mill, then put them in a bowl.

Add the paprika, cayenne, garlic, and salt. Stir in the olive oil and vinegar. The harissa oil will keep in the fridge for a week or two.

Fragrant Lamb with Prunes and Almonds

It's too bad lamb shanks have become so chic they're now expensive. You could easily make this tagine with boneless lamb shoulder cut into half-pound chunks. It would be just as delicious and less pricey. SERVES 6

FOR THE TAGINE

6 pounds lamb shanks or
   4 pounds boneless lamb
   shoulder, trimmed of fat
Salt and pepper
2 tablespoons butter
2 medium onions, thickly sliced
Pinch of saffron threads
6 garlic cloves, chopped
One 2-inch chunk ginger,
   peeled and slivered
1 small cinnamon stick
1 teaspoon coriander seeds

1 teaspoon cumin seeds
1 tablespoon powdered ginger
2 teaspoons cayenne
1 cup golden raisins
2 cups pitted prunes
4 cups chicken broth or water
1 cup tomato puree

FOR THE GARNISH

1 tablespoon butter
1 cup blanched whole almonds
Large pinch of salt
Small pinch of sugar

Preheat the oven to 325°F. Season the lamb generously with salt and pepper, and set aside.

Melt the butter in a large skillet. Add the onions, sprinkle with a little salt, and crumble the saffron over them. Stew the onions gently for about 5 minutes, or until slightly softened. Remove from the heat and stir in the garlic, fresh ginger, cinnamon stick, coriander and cumin seeds, powdered ginger, and cayenne. Add the raisins and half the prunes.

Put the lamb in a Dutch oven or deep-sided baking dish and spread the onion mixture over the meat. Add the broth or water and the tomato puree, and cover the pot with foil and a tight-fitting lid. Bake for about 2 hours, or until the meat is meltingly tender.

Remove the foil and lid, add the second cup of prunes, and submerge them in the liquid. Raise the heat to 400°F and return the lamb to the oven, uncovered, for about 15 minutes to let the meat brown a bit. Remove the pot from the oven and let it rest for 10 minutes or so.

Skim off any fat from the surface of the tagine. If the sauce seems thin, pour into a saucepan and reduce. The tagine is ready to serve, but it will also reheat perfectly, so you can make it today to serve tomorrow. (The sauce will mature beautifully in the refrigerator overnight.)

Just before you're ready to serve the tagine, fry the almonds for garnish: Heat the butter in a small skillet over medium heat and fry the almonds gently, stirring occasionally. When the almonds are golden, drain them on paper towels and sprinkle them with the salt and sugar.

To serve, transfer the stew to a large platter and scatter the fried almonds over the lamb.

[VARIATION] A RABBIT TAGINE

You can make the stew exactly the same way with a couple of small rabbits or one large chicken, cut up. Just plan on a shorter cooking time, and check the meat at 1½ hours.

Blood Oranges and Pomegranates
with Orange Flower Water

The blood orange is the brilliant red-fleshed fruit of the Mediterranean. Originally imported from Morocco, Tunisia, Spain, and southern Italy, blood oranges are increasingly cultivated in the United States. To me, the fruit has an almost tropical taste, which is so welcome in winter and especially refreshing after the lamb tagine. The oranges are not only beautiful to look at, but also satisfying to eat.

The pomegranate is so elegant you could imagine it growing on velvet-covered branches. In truth, the fruits grow on scruffy bushes, a fact that somehow escaped me until I saw them for myself in Morocco, poking out of the brush like so many hedge apples. For dessert one night, I was served a simple bowl of glistening ruby pomegranate seeds. It was a totally sensuous gesture. A spoonful of those ripe seeds was like nectar.

1 large pomegranate	Orange flower water
6 blood oranges	A little sugar if necessary

Cut the pomegranate into quarters and invert each quarter over a large bowl to force out the seeds.

Peel the blood oranges with a serrated knife. Working over the bowl, cut between the membranes to section each orange, letting the segments drop into the bowl. Before discarding the membranes, give them a squeeze over the bowl to capture every bit of juice.

Mix the oranges, juice, and pomegranate seeds together, and add a splash of orange flower water. Taste, and if the juice is too tart, add a little sugar. Chill for at least an hour.

Serve in small bowls.

Of Buckwheat and Mussels

Buckwheat Galettes with Ham and Cheese
Mâche Salad
Mussels Marinière, Brittany-Style
Apple Compote
Butter Cookies

It was the great *canicule,* a heat wave so severe that the sidewalks in Paris were still steaming at midnight. We just had to get some fresh air. So Randal and I and the two dogs, Arturo and Ajax, hightailed it out of town in a rented air-conditioned car. First, we headed south, only to discover that everyone else had, too. Then we made a big loop and headed northwest to the farthest reaches of Brittany's Atlantic coast, and to the north coast of Normandy—the land of apples, butter, buckwheat, and mussels.

We found ourselves on a small island just off the mainland of Brittany, the Ile de Bréhat, known for its ancient buckwheat mill. Situated right on the sea, the mill was ingeniously calibrated to work with the tides; as the tides moved, so did the mill. The Moulin de Birlot had been converted into a museum and was run by one old guy who wanted to preserve the history of the place. He was only too happy to show us how buckwheat was ground. Although the French call it *blé noir,* and some tourist menus translate it

incorrectly as black wheat, buckwheat is a grain that comes from a leafy plant, and is not at all a grass like wheat.

So it was that summer in Brittany, on that island where no cars were allowed and you had to take a ten-minute ferry from the mainland, that I became truly enamored of the buckwheat galette.

A galette is a large, savory crêpe more common there than pizza, filled with mushrooms, spinach, tomatoes, or anything at all, really. The best, to me, is the ham-and-cheese-filled galette, with an egg in the middle. The nomenclature is a bit confusing. Galettes are made with buckwheat flour and are almost always savory, while crêpes are usually sweet and always made with white flour. There's something so wonderfully intense about the nutty, roasty flavor of buckwheat, it's a shame not to use it more (buckwheat is also the stuff of the acclaimed Japanese soba noodles). In a restaurant, galettes are baked on a big, round griddle and then the edges are folded in so that the circle makes a large square. Served as a main course, a galette owns the plate. At home I sometimes make smaller ones or cut them into wedges to eat with salad. Because buckwheat flour has no gluten, I add some white flour to the batter, but I try to keep it as buckwheaty as possible.

Mussels in most of France are a bit like fast food. It's awful to get them in a tourist restaurant, where they are drowned in cheap wine, too much garlic, and bad tomato sauce, and inevitably called "Provençal" on the menu. Worse are *moules frites,* so served because french fries sell. But today even French french fries are all frozen anyway—nobody makes their own *frites* anymore. (And I'd rather eat good mussels with good bread than with fries.)

Up in mussel country, though, it's a completely different story. In the little port of Barfleur, a very old fishing village in Normandy, a fresh mussel is incredible. Tiny bouchot mussels, born in the waters of that northwestern coast, are farmed on wooden posts (*bouchots*) and harvested at low tide. There's not a fresher dish of mussels to be had—these mussels have never traveled. A large pot of steamed mussels can be found in any little restaurant in Barfleur (indeed, in most coastal towns of the area), accompanied by a bottle of local cider, at a very reasonable price. Some places offer, for variety's sake, curried mussels, or mussels with cream and Calvados, but for mussels this fresh, sweet, and briny, the best preparation is *à la marinière,* with just a splash of white wine and a few aromatics.

Mussel season in France is from July to November, due to several factors including water temperature and type of mussel, so the lucky French get to enjoy them during the summer holidays as well as in rainy weather. In the United States the season for most mussels is late fall to early spring, so we think of mussels as cold-weather fare. Nearly all mussels that come to market today are farmed, a practice that, unlike many other aquaculture ventures, is environmentally sound. For food, the mussels simply filter seawater for the plankton and other nutrients they thrive on. The industry is well managed and highly regulated. Prince Edward Island in Canada supplies a majority of the mussels in America. Mussels are farmed in parts of New England too, and on the West Coast in Washington and California. It's fun to collect wild mussels, but you need to be certain you're taking them from approved waters. Check ahead with your local department of fish and wildlife.

Try to buy your mussels the day they arrive at the fish market and eat them immediately. The fresher they are, the better they are

Buckwheat Galettes with Ham and Cheese

Buckwheat galettes are great for a light lunch or, as in this menu, a first course served with Mâche Salad (recipe follows).

1 cup buckwheat flour
½ cup all-purpose flour
2 eggs
2½ cups whole milk
½ teaspoon salt

¼ cup roasted buckwheat groats (kasha), finely ground in a coffee grinder
About 2 tablespoons butter, melted
6 slices good-quality cooked ham
2 cups grated Comté or Gruyère

Whisk together the flours, eggs, milk, salt, and groats in a mixing bowl until well combined. Put the batter in the refrigerator for at least 2 hours; overnight is best.

Heat a crêpe pan or a well-seasoned cast-iron pan, about 8 inches in diameter, over medium-high heat. With a piece of paper towel, rub a little butter in the pan, then quickly ladle in about ⅓ cup batter. Swirl the pan to spread the batter. Let the galette brown on one side, then flip it over with a spatula. (When you become an expert, you can just grab the edge of the galette with your fingertips to turn it.) Remove the galette from the pan and set it aside while you continue to make the rest of the galettes.

To fill the galettes, lay each one top side down, place a slice of ham on top and sprinkle with a generous pinch of grated cheese, and fold over to make a half-moon. Put the filled galettes in one layer on a baking sheet.

Just before serving, preheat the oven to 400°F. Drizzle the galettes with a little melted butter. Pop them into the oven until they are crisp and the cheese is melted. Serve immediately, with the salad.

Mâche Salad

Mâche is as common in Europe as butter lettuce is here, though it's becoming more available in this country. In Switzerland, they make a wonderful mâche salad with a little bit of chopped egg, and that's the inspiration for this one. If you have difficulty finding mâche, use a combination of curly endive and baby spinach.

1 pound mâche rosettes

1 small shallot, finely diced

1 tablespoon sherry vinegar

1 tablespoon red wine vinegar

Salt and pepper

1 teaspoon Dijon mustard

3 tablespoons olive oil

1 tablespoon walnut oil

2 eggs, hard-cooked

It's tricky to wash mâche; sand and grit love to hide in all the whorled leaves, and you need to pay special attention to the rosettes. Pick over the whole batch with a paring knife and trim the root ends carefully, leaving the rosettes intact. Trim off any yellow leaves. Swish the rosettes in a large basin of cold water, and use your fingers to dislodge any sand and grit. Repeat several times, until the mâche is clean. Lift the mâche into a colander and drain well, then wrap in a kitchen towel and refrigerate until ready to use.

To make the vinaigrette, put the shallot in a small bowl and add the vinegars and salt and pepper. Let sit for 5 minutes, then whisk in the mustard, olive oil, and walnut oil. (The dressing can be made several hours in advance.)

When you're ready to dress the salad, put the greens in a big salad bowl. Sprinkle lightly with salt, pour the vinaigrette over the greens, and toss gently to coat all the leaves. Roughly chop the eggs and scatter them over the top.

Mussels Marinière, Brittany-Style

Despite the fact that most mussel places offer *moules* seven ways, including curried mussels and mussels with cream and Calvados, for me the best way is still the plainest way: simply steamed with white wine with just a few aromatics to enhance the briny broth. There's nothing easier or more satisfying for a casual dinner than to just bring the whole pot of mussels to the table and let everyone eat their fill, tossing the shells into a big bowl. The right way to eat a mussel is with your fingers, using a shell to pluck out the sweet meat and as a spoon for the broth. SERVES 4 TO 6

1½ pounds mussels per person
4 tablespoons butter
1 medium onion or 2 large
   shallots, finely diced
Salt and pepper
4 garlic cloves, smashed to a paste
   with a little salt

1 large thyme sprig
1 bay leaf
2 cups dry white wine
A small bunch of parsley
2 crisp baguettes

First clean the mussels by putting them in a large basin of cold water. Give them a few swishes to loosen any sand or grit. Inspect each mussel and pull off the little "beard" that attaches them to rocks or rope. All of this is accomplished quickly, since most farmed mussels are quite clean when they come to market. Put the mussels in a colander and cover them with a damp towel until you're ready to cook them.

In a large deep heavy-bottomed pot with a lid—a big enameled cast-iron pot is perfect, or two pots if you don't have one big enough—melt the butter over medium heat. Add the onion or shallots and a little salt and pepper and stew gently until softened, about 5 minutes.

Add the garlic, thyme sprig, bay leaf, wine, and mussels, cover, and steam the mussels over high heat for about 10 minutes, until they are all open. You'll need to remove the lid and stir the mussels around several times to distribute them so they cook evenly.

While the mussels are steaming, chop the parsley, so it's fresh. When the mussels are done, toss in the chopped parsley and stir.

Bring the steaming pot to the table and ladle out a big bowlful for each person. Put the baguettes on the table. Encourage sopping.

Apple Compote

Apples are synonymous with Normandy and Brittany, and cider is the drink of choice with both galettes and mussels. Everybody makes their own cider. It is very lightly alcoholic, with just a few little bubbles, and tastes fresh and delicious. A tiny glass of Calvados, the local brandy made from apples, makes a pleasant little digestif.

Compôte de pommes sounds fancy, but it's just good, homemade applesauce that really tastes of apple. It's not too sweet, and it has just a touch of perfume from the lemon slice. This method works with any kind of apple.

6 large apples	**1 lemon slice**
½ cup sugar	**1 cup water**

Peel, quarter, and core the apples. Put them in a heavy-bottomed pot, add the sugar, lemon slice, and water, and bring to a boil, then reduce to a simmer. Cover and let cook for about 20 minutes, until the apples are soft. Turn off the heat and let the apples sit in the pot, covered, until cool.

When the apples have cooled, mash them a bit with a wooden spoon, but leave them chunky. Stir to incorporate the juices, and serve at room temperature.

Butter Cookies

Though I usually cook with more olive oil than butter, since we're in this region, butter rules! And it's such good butter. In France, you can find really good store-bought butter cookies, but in the States you have to make your own.

French butter has a higher fat content and a lower moisture content. It makes a real difference in cookies and pastry—worth the expense. MAKES ABOUT 4 DOZEN COOKIES

½ pound (2 sticks) best-quality
   unsalted butter, softened
¾ cup sugar
2 egg yolks

½ teaspoon salt
½ teaspoon vanilla extract
2 cups all-purpose flour

In a large mixing bowl, cream the butter with the sugar, using an electric mixer. Add the egg yolks, salt, and vanilla extract and beat well. Work in the flour to make a soft dough.

Divide the dough in half and shape into 2 logs, about 1 inch in diameter. Wrap with plastic wrap and chill for about an hour, until the logs are firm enough to slice.

Preheat the oven to 350°F. Slice the dough into ½-inch-thick disks and transfer to parchment-lined baking sheets, spacing the cookies about an inch apart. Bake for 12 to 15 minutes, until the cookies have turned golden. Cool on a rack.

Bring Back Tongue

Greens on Toast
Bollito Misto of Tongue and Brisket with Two Sauces
Walnut and Pine Nut Drops

As a child, I was a spinach and liver fan—and among the other things that I did not find repulsive was tongue. Not that my mother was an adventuresome cook, but (beef) tongue was a normal thing in our house. You just put it in the pot and let it go. We would eat it with applesauce. Cold applesauce. Nobody was grossed out or squeamish the way they seem to be today. And tongue made a great sandwich the next day on white bread with Miracle Whip.

Tongue goes in and out of favor in the American kitchen. There's more than beef tongue to enjoy. Veal tongue, like veal itself, is more delicate than beef, especially with a light mushroom sauce. Or cold with mustard and pickles. It's the star of the renowned French *tête de veau,* served with sauce gribiche. Lamb's tongues are absolutely delicious—one per person, simmered gently in an aromatic broth and sliced thin and served with a vinaigrette, warm or cold. Can I just say, "Oh, my lord!"

Pork tongues don't come to market often, but if you can find them, they're perfectly delicious. Classic Italian *testa,* the Italian version of head cheese, has lots of pork tongue and orange zest. Like pork, tongue can be

corned and smoked. Both preparations enhance the meat's lusciousness. Unlike other offal, tongue is easy to love. There's no strong flavor or texture that you have to overcome to enjoy it. And tongue is not really an organ, it's just another piece of meat.

In general, all tongue is prepared in a similar fashion: Salt it overnight, then simmer gently, and serve warm or cool. The only challenge in preparing tongue is the peeling. A tongue will never peel until it is completely, completely cooked, but once cooked, it almost peels itself.

If you don't feel like cooking, every good taco truck has *tacos de lengua,* beef tongue tacos with sweet onions and chiles. They are over-the-top delicious—the best thing on the taco menu.

Katz's Delicatessen on Manhattan's Lower East Side still serves a half tongue, half pastrami sandwich. But there are not many places left where you can count on getting a slice of hot tongue and a boiled potato, even in New York.

Greens on Toast

Because the bollito is a very hearty meal, you want only a tiny taste of a first course, and since you're going to be having mostly meat, it should preferably be vegetables. So you could prepare a plate of sliced fresh fennel and radishes with salt and lemon—Italian-style crudités. Or make these greens crostini.

¼ cup olive oil, plus extra for the toasts
4 garlic cloves, finely chopped
½ teaspoon red pepper flakes
4 anchovy fillets, rinsed and chopped

4 cups rapini (broccoli rabe), or a mixture of chard, mustard greens, and full-grown spinach leaves, coarsely chopped
Salt and pepper
1 baguette, preferably day-old, sliced into ¼-inch-thick rounds
Lemon wedges

Preheat the oven to 375°F. Heat the oil in a wide skillet over medium heat. Add the garlic, red pepper flakes, and anchovies and let them sizzle without browning. Add all the greens to the skillet, with any water from washing still clinging to the leaves, season with salt and pepper, stir well, and put on the lid. Let the greens steam and wilt, stirring once or twice, for about 5 minutes.

Meanwhile, make the toasts. Paint the slices very lightly with olive oil, spread them in one layer on a baking sheet, and bake until barely browned, about 10 minutes. Cool the toasts.

When the greens are wilted but still bright green, transfer them to a platter to cool to room temperature. Taste and adjust the seasoning.

To serve, put a forkful of greens on each toast and squeeze a bit of lemon over the top, or have people make their own. (If you have leftover greens, add them to a pasta or bean soup.)

Bollito Misto of Tongue and Brisket with Two Sauces

There is, of course, the grand *bollito misto* of legendary Italian restaurants—where an elegant trolley of boiled meats and vegetables is wheeled over to your table—but this is very much a home version. You need another meat besides tongue, here brisket, to make the great broth that bollito is famous for. Bollito is always made with leftovers in mind, so this recipe will serve 4 to 6—and give you plenty of broth for risotto or meat for ravioli filling or a next-day salad.

1 beef tongue, about 3 pounds	6 quarts water
One 4-pound beef brisket	2 pounds medium Yellow Finn
Salt and pepper	potatoes, peeled
1 large onion, peeled, halved,	1 small bunch parsley, leaves
and stuck with 1 clove	chopped
1 large carrot, peeled and halved	Coarse salt
1 small celery stalk	Dijon mustard
1 bay leaf	Caper Sauce (recipe follows)
1 thyme sprig	Red Pepper Sauce (recipe follows)
6 black peppercorns	

Begin preparing the bollito the night before: Season the tongue and brisket generously with salt and pepper. Cover them and refrigerate overnight.

The next day, rinse the tongue and beef with cool water and put in a large heavy-bottomed soup pot. Add the onion, carrot, celery, bay leaf, thyme, and peppercorns, cover with the water, and bring to a hard boil. Then turn down the heat to a low simmer and simmer very gently, spooning off any scum that rises to the surface, for about 3 hours. The brisket should be done at about the 3-hour mark—tender but not falling apart. Take it out of the pot and let it cool to room temperature.

While the brisket may be tender, the tongue might still have a way to go. Take it from the pot and put it on a cutting board. The only way to tell if the tongue is done: use a small paring knife to test if it is peelable—can the white skin be easily removed? If not, return the tongue to the pot for a little while longer, then remove it and peel while it is still warm. Discard the skin and allow the tongue to cool to room temperature.

In a large saucepan, cover the potatoes with water, add a spoonful of salt, bring to a boil, and boil for 15 minutes, or until tender. Drain and let sit for 5 minutes or more, covered.

Meanwhile, strain the broth and degrease it. Taste and adjust the seasoning.

Both the brisket and tongue may need a slight trimming of fat and gristle. Slice as much tongue as you intend to serve crosswise into thin slices. Ditto with the beef. Warm the meat in the broth.

Remove the sliced meat from the broth and arrange it on a generous platter. Surround with the potatoes, sprinkle liberally with the parsley, carry it to the table, and enjoy. Serve everyone a small cup of broth to sip immediately. Then pass the platter, with the coarse salt, mustard, and caper and red pepper sauces.

{VARIATION} TONGUE AND/OR BRISKET VINAIGRETTE WITH CAPERS

Depending on the state of your leftovers, both the tongue and brisket are delicious the next day sliced thin and dressed with an assertive vinaigrette. Nearly any vinaigrette you can think up will work, especially mustard or anchovy, or a simple mix of olive oil, capers, lemon juice, and a lot of chopped parsley.

Caper Sauce

2 tablespoons Dijon mustard
2 teaspoons capers, rinsed
1 cup olive oil

2 tablespoons each coarsely
    chopped parsley, basil, and
    chives
Generous pinch of cayenne
Salt and pepper to taste

Put all the ingredients in a blender and blend on high speed until the herbs are well pureed, the sauce emulsified and thick. Taste and adjust the seasonings. Pour into a small serving bowl. (The sauce can be made an hour or so ahead.)

Red Pepper Sauce

1 cup good-quality canned
    tomatoes, drained
1 garlic clove
½ teaspoon cayenne

Salt and pepper
1 sweet red pepper, roasted,
    or ½ cup jarred roasted peppers
¼ cup olive oil

Put all the ingredients in a blender and blend on high speed to a thick puree. Taste and adjust the seasonings. Pour into a small serving bowl and serve.

Walnut and Pine Nut Drops

These cookies are a variation on the classic *brutti-ma-buoni* (ugly-but-good). It's important to use the freshest walnuts and pine nuts you can find. Toast the nuts separately on a dry baking sheet and let them cool before proceeding. MAKES ABOUT 2 DOZEN COOKIES

2 cups walnuts, halves or pieces, lightly toasted

3 tablespoons all-purpose flour

¾ cup granulated sugar

¾ cup brown sugar

½ cup pine nuts, lightly toasted but not browned

4 egg whites

½ teaspoon salt

Preheat the oven to 350°F. Line a cookie sheet with parchment paper.

Put the walnuts in a food processor. Add the flour and granulated sugar and pulse for about 30 seconds, taking care to leave the walnuts in coarse pebble-sized chunks. Transfer the mixture to a bowl and stir in the brown sugar and pine nuts.

In a separate bowl, whisk the egg whites with the salt until frothy. Fold the egg whites into the nut mixture and stir with a wooden spoon to incorporate.

With a teaspoon, drop the batter into rough cookie shapes about 1 inch apart on the baking sheet.

Bake until barely browned, about 10 minutes. Cool on a rack.

Simple Feasts for a Long Table

There are occasions throughout the year, usually built around some solstice or other, when a celebration is called for. And it is always *someone's* birthday. Instead of having a so-so (and quickly forgotten) meal at a restaurant, or engaging a caterer to bring the dinner to you, cook it! The very gesture of setting up a long table is a festive act: this is something special! And the menu needn't be complicated. In fact, it shouldn't be. The fact of gathering is what counts. And it's much easier than you might think.

The way I think about it, the bigger the group, the simpler the food. It's an excellent idea to ask a couple of friends to help in the kitchen and with serving, or even hire some assistance with the dishes. For ease of service, I've planned it so the main course in these menus is the sit-down course. I think it's unnecessarily complicated to serve a first course of a soup or a salad with all the attendant bowls and plates. So, in each menu I've suggested a stand-up appetizer as a first course for nibbling. It could be as simple as bowls of olives, radishes, and almonds.

As for the end of the meal, I've suggested simple desserts, but I never have qualms about farming out dessert. People are always asking what they should bring. If you have a friend who loves to make desserts, make sure she's invited. If the occasion's a birthday or anniversary, ask someone to make a cake. Or serve a voluptuous platter of seasonal fruits: strawberries in the spring, stone fruit and berries in summer, grapes and pears and apples in autumn, tangerines in winter.

spring feast
A PERFECT SUCKLING PIG
Artichoke Antipasto

Roast Suckling Pig Italian-Style with Roman Potatoes

Salad of Fennel and Bitter Greens

Almond Cookies and a Bowl of Cherries

summer feast
HOW TO SPICE A GOAT
Lobster Salpicón with Avocado

Long-Simmered Cabrito

Green Rice

Inside-Out Mangoes

fall feast
TURKEY DECONSTRUCTED
Roasted and Braised Turkey with Gravy

Chicken Liver and Apple Stuffing

Spicy Cranberry Chutney

winter feast
AUSPICIOUS AND DELICIOUS
Hair of the Dog, Salty Dog, and Other Grapefruit Drinks

Relish Plate

Quick Bread-and-Butter Pickles

Crab-Stuffed Deviled Eggs

Black-eyed Peas with Ham Hocks and Bacon

Corn Sticks

Lemon Curd Shortbread with Candied Kumquat

A Perfect Suckling Pig

Artichoke Antipasto
Roast Suckling Pig Italian-Style with Roman Potatoes
Salad of Fennel and Bitter Greens
Almond Cookies and a Bowl of Cherries

Who doesn't love suckling pig? It's considered special-occasion food from San Juan to Napoli.

This menu could go so many ways, with any number of accompaniments and seasonings. You want to season the pig, but you don't want to overwhelm its young succulence. In fact, this little pig needs so little help, salt and pepper would do just fine. Chinese five-spice powder might inspire accompaniments of roasted yams, steamed rice, and garlicky Asian greens. Cubans like to marinate their pig in citrus juices and garlic and serve it with beans and fried plantains. Italian-style suckling pig, like this one, is scented with rosemary and fennel seeds and served with crisp roasted potatoes and a salad of sweet fennel and bitter greens.

In general, a young pig will feed its weight in people—i.e., a 15- to 20-pound pig will be ample for 15 to 20 people. These small pigs are usually available from good Italian, Chinese, or Latino butchers, but you'll need to order in advance.

Artichoke Antipasto

The difference between these marinated artichokes and commercial artichokes in jars (too heavy on vinegar, drowning in mediocre oil) is light-years.

5 pounds baby artichokes, about 2 dozen

Grated zest and juice of 1 lemon

½ cup olive oil

Salt and pepper

A small glass of dry white wine

3 or 4 thyme sprigs

4 small garlic cloves, chopped

A generous pinch of red pepper flakes

1 bunch parsley, leaves roughly chopped

To prepare the baby artichokes, cut off the tops and remove a few outer leaves from each to reveal the pale green centers. Trim the stem ends with a paring knife. Halve the artichokes lengthwise and put them in a bowl of cool water. Squeeze in the lemon juice and reserve until you're ready to cook them.

Heat the olive oil in a large skillet (not cast iron). Drain the artichokes. Add them to the pan and season well with salt and pepper, then add the wine and thyme and simmer uncovered, stirring occasionally, until the artichokes are tender when you test them with a fork, about 10 minutes.

Add the garlic and red pepper flakes, stir, and cook for a minute. Off the heat, stir in the lemon zest and chopped parsley. Transfer the artichokes to a low, wide serving dish and let cool to room temperature.

When the artichokes are cool, taste for salt and lemon juice. They should be very well seasoned, because fresh baby artichokes can be sweet and need salt and acidity to balance the flavor. Cover and leave at room temperature until ready to serve, up to several hours hence.

When your guests arrive, place the artichokes on a side table as the heart of your antipasto. Surround with bowls of olives, crisp radishes, sliced fresh mozzarella, a few slices of prosciutto and salami, and perhaps a focaccia (see page 167).

Roast Suckling Pig Italian-Style with Roman Potatoes

A suckling pig benefits greatly from seasoning overnight, but good luck to anyone trying to find room to fit a whole pig in the refrigerator. A fine way to accomplish this is to put the seasoned pig in a big plastic bag and store it in a camping cooler with a bag of ice. In the same vein, make sure you have a roasting pan big enough to hold the whole pig and that your oven, with all but one shelf removed, will accommodate both pig and pan.

1 young pig, 15 to 20 pounds

Salt and pepper

1 tablespoon fennel seeds, crushed in a mortar

½ cup rosemary leaves

½ cup sage leaves and tender stems

2 heads garlic, broken into cloves, peeled, and roughly chopped

1 tablespoon olive oil

Roman Potatoes (recipe follows)

Rinse the pig, pat it dry, and lay it on its side in a large roasting pan. Season it generously on both sides and inside the cavity with salt, pepper, and the fennel seeds.

Mix the rosemary, sage, and garlic together with a generous amount of coarsely ground black pepper and the olive oil, and smear the mixture inside the cavity.

With a heavy-duty needle and thread or butcher's twine, sew up the cavity with a few quick loops, just to hold it together. Configure the pig with all 4 legs pointing forward and transfer it from the roasting pan to a plastic bag. Pack it into a cooler with a bag of ice and leave it overnight.

The next day, remove the pig from the cooler and bag and put it in the roasting pan. Let it come to room temperature, probably a couple of hours.

Preheat the oven to 400°F. Pour an inch of water into the roasting pan and put the pig in the oven. After 30 minutes, reduce the oven to 325°F, and continue roasting, basting occasionally with the juices in the pan (you can use a bunch of rosemary as a basting brush). If any part of the pig (like the snout, tail, or ears) begins to get too brown, wrap a piece of foil around it. At 2 hours, check the thick part of the leg with your instant-read thermometer: it should read 150°F, and the juices should run clear.

Pierce the skin in a few places behind the shoulders to release a little of the fat to help crisp the skin. Turn up the heat to 500°F to crackle the skin for about 10 minutes (the time will depend on the heat of your oven). The skin should be a rich mahogany color. Remove the pig from the oven and let it rest in the roasting pan for 20 to 30 minutes.

Transfer the pig to a large carving board. Reserve the roasting pan with its juices for the potatoes. You can carve the pig as you would a turkey, taking pieces off the carcass, but I prefer to separate the pig into large pieces: the forelegs, the hind legs, and the center. You're not going for perfectly carved thin slices. The ideal is rough chunks of meat with some crisp skin attached. I use a sharp heavy Chinese cleaver, making it easy to take out the midsection, which contains the loins and ribs, cutting right through the crisp skin and tender bones. Now cut the midsection into small pieces. Serve the meat right from the cutting board—that way, you can cut more meat as you need it—and pass the potatoes.

Roman Potatoes

These potatoes are parboiled, then roasted with the pan juices of the suckling pig, which makes them the crispiest and best roasted potatoes on earth. Choose small potatoes like Yellow Finn, Yukon Gold, or Bintje. Plan on a half pound per person. There will not be leftovers!

{CONTINUED}

Peel your potatoes, then boil them ahead of time in a large pot of salted water for about 10 minutes; they should still be rather firm. Spread them out to cool.

Turn the oven down to 400°F. While the pig is resting, put the potatoes in the roasting pan in one layer. Turn them in the juices with a wooden spoon to coat them evenly. You may need to add a splash of water.

Put the pan in the oven and roast the potatoes. They should be brown and crispy in about 15 to 20 minutes. Shake the pan but try not to move the potatoes until they're well browned. Pile them on a warm platter, sprinkle with chopped parsley, and serve.

Salad of Fennel and Bitter Greens

Fennel is probably my favorite cool-weather vegetable. Hold out for tender, young fennel that looks alive and freshly picked, with nice pale green bulbs. It's amazing how fast fennel loses its flavor as it ages. You want that delicious, juicy snap. Fennel and pork work perfectly together. The sweet fennel in the salad echoes the fennel-seed seasoning of the pork. And it's a perfect foil for radicchio and other slightly bitter greens.

FOR THE VINAIGRETTE

1 large shallot, finely diced

1 tablespoon red wine vinegar

2 tablespoons sherry vinegar

Salt and pepper

2 garlic cloves, smashed to a paste
  with a little salt

1 teaspoon Dijon mustard

½ cup olive oil

FOR THE SALAD

6 fennel bulbs, very fresh

Salt and pepper

Juice of ½ lemon

8 to 10 large handfuls assorted
  bitter greens, such as radicchio,
  castelfranco, and escarole, curly
  or otherwise, washed

Make the vinaigrette an hour or two ahead if you wish: Macerate the shallot in the vinegars with a little salt in a small bowl. Whisk together with the garlic and mustard, then whisk in the olive oil. Grind in a little fresh pepper, taste, and adjust the seasoning. Set the vinaigrette aside.

I believe most people don't trim fennel properly. The outer layer of the bulb can be very tough and fibrous, and it really must be removed. And, except for very young fennel bulbs, the core should be removed as well. First cut off the stalks, then slice off a little bit of the root end—this will allow you to peel away the tough outer layer. Put the trimmed fennel bulbs in a bowl of cold water until you are ready to use them.

To make the salad, cut the fennel bulbs lengthwise in half, and notch out the cores with a paring knife if they seem at all tough. Slice the fennel bulbs thin (but not paper-thin) with a sharp knife or a mandoline. Put the slices in a large salad bowl and cover with a damp towel. (Do this only up to 10 minutes before serving, or the fennel will begin to turn brown and lose its fresh-sliced flavor.)

To dress the salad, season the sliced fennel with salt and pepper and lemon juice. Pour in enough of the vinaigrette to dress the fennel lightly. Add the salad greens and another light sprinkling of salt. Gently mix the leaves with the fennel so the leaves are well coated and the fennel is nicely distributed throughout. Add more vinaigrette if necessary.

Almond Cookies and a Bowl of Cherries

These little almond cookies taste so very Italian, and they're everything I want in a cookie—crisp exterior, moist center, slightly chewy. Accompany them with a huge bowl of cherries. It's a real sign of spring when cherries show up at the market. Look for cherries with fresh stems and firm shiny flesh.

1 cup raw almonds

½ teaspoon baking powder

Pinch of salt

¾ pound good-quality almond
  paste

1 egg white, beaten

½ teaspoon vanilla extract

Powdered sugar

Preheat the oven to 350°F. Grind the almonds to a fine powder in a spice grinder or a food processor. Put the almonds in a mixing bowl and stir in the baking powder and salt. Add the almond paste, egg white, and vanilla and mix well until a nice dough forms.

Roll the dough into 2 dozen little balls, about 1 inch in diameter. Put the little almond balls on a parchment-lined baking sheet, about 1 inch apart.

Sprinkle the cookies with powdered sugar and bake for 12 to 14 minutes. The cookies will puff and crackle a bit, and they'll be done when they turn just barely golden. Cool them on a rack.

How to Spice a Goat

Lobster Salpicón with Avocado
Long-Simmered Cabrito
Green Rice
Inside-Out Mangoes

I went to a party once, way out in the country outside Mexico City. The hostess, a well-known Mexican chef, had set an enormous long table in the courtyard of an old hacienda. We feasted all night on traditional regional cuisine. Ringing the outdoor dining area were little food concessions, each with its specialty: ceviche, tamales, camarones. One of the best offerings was called *barbacoa,* kid goat simmered in an enormous kettle set over a wood fire. *Barbacoa* sounds like "barbecue," but it is really a slow braise, a simmered version of the spit-roasted or pit-cooked *cabrito* popular all over Mexico. The advantages of cooking the goat in a pot are twofold: you get the succulent meat as well as the delicious broth it's cooked in.

This simmered goat stew was one of the best things I've ever eaten, and now it is one of my favorite things to cook. It's perfect for a crowd, and leftovers (if there are any) are welcome the next day for making *tacos al pastor.*

If you can't get a kid goat, substitute larger cuts of mature goat or lamb. You can also adapt the recipe and make the dish with pork or chicken.

Lobster Salpicón with Avocado

Salpicón is a Mexican cross between a salsa and a vinaigrette, very fresh, bright, and crunchy. This could be served as a stand-up appetizer the way I suggest here—with half avocados filled with lobster, to be eaten with a spoon—or folded into little tortillas for stand-up tacos, or it could be plated as a first course. You can easily substitute shrimp or crabmeat for the lobster.

1½ pounds freshly cooked lobster
  meat, roughly chopped
1 large sweet onion, finely diced
2 sweet red peppers, finely diced
2 bunches radishes, finely diced
1 large cucumber, peeled and
  finely diced
4 Roma (plum) tomatoes, finely
  diced

1 or 2 serrano chiles, very finely
  chopped
Salt and pepper
2 tablespoons olive oil
Juice of 2 limes
1 small bunch cilantro, leaves
  and tender stems chopped
6 firm but ripe avocados,
  halved and pitted
Lime wedges

You can prepare all the ingredients ahead and keep them cold, but don't dress the lobster until you're ready to serve it.

Put the lobster and all the chopped vegetables (including the chiles) in a large mixing bowl. Season with salt and pepper. Add the olive oil and lime juice. Toss carefully and well. Taste and adjust the seasonings. Add the cilantro.

Spoon the salpicón into the avocado halves and serve them with lime wedges.

Long-Simmered Cabrito

Like any great stew, this dish benefits from overnight seasoning. Even better, cook it the day before you serve it.

6 dried ancho chiles

10 cups water

¼ cup cider vinegar or rice wine
vinegar

2 small heads garlic, broken into
cloves and peeled

One 12- to 15-pound kid
goat, cut into 6 or 8 pieces
(legs, shoulders, midsection)

Salt and pepper

2 bay leaves

1 cinnamon stick

A few whole cloves

2 tablespoons cumin seeds,
toasted and ground

Pinch of dried oregano

4 large onions, finely diced

FOR SERVING

1 bunch cilantro, leaves and tender
stems chopped

1 small onion, finely diced

Lime wedges

Corn tortillas

Heat a cast-iron pan over medium heat and toast the chiles just until they puff up a little and become fragrant. Remove the chiles from the pan and take out the seeds. Put the chiles in a small saucepan, cover with 2 cups of the water, and boil for 5 minutes.

Put the chiles, cooking liquid, and vinegar in a blender along with the garlic. Puree the mixture and cool.

Season the goat meat generously with salt and pepper. Smear the chile paste all over the pieces. Wrap the meat and refrigerate overnight.

The next day, preheat the oven to 325°F. Put the meat in a deep roasting pan. Add the remaining 8 cups water, the bay leaves, cinnamon stick, cloves, cumin, oregano, and onions. Cover, put in the oven, and cook for about 3 hours, until the meat is falling from the bone.

Remove the pan from the oven. Pour off the liquid into a large bowl. Let it sit for a minute, then skim off any fat on the surface.

Tear the meat into rough pieces, then pour the broth over.

Ladle the meat and broth into shallow soup bowls along with a spoonful of green rice (next recipe). Garnish wth the cilantro and diced onion, and serve with lime wedges and warm tortillas.

Green Rice

This kind of rice, cooked in an earthenware *cazuela,* is made all over Mexico. It is green or red, depending on whether you make it with tomatillos or tomatoes. The rice gains flavor if you cook it in chicken broth, but you can make it vegetarian as well.

2 tablespoons olive oil

1 large onion, finely diced

2 cups long-grain white rice

1 cup chopped cilantro

2 or 3 garlic cloves

10 medium tomatillos, husked, rinsed, and halved

1 serrano chile, roughly chopped

2 teaspoons salt

About 2 cups chicken broth or water

FOR GARNISH

Chopped cilantro

Slivered scallions

Preheat the oven to 350°F. Warm the olive oil in a 15-inch-diameter cazuela or a wide heavy-bottomed ovenproof pot over medium heat. Add the onion and turn up the heat a little to let it lightly fry, soften, and color a bit. Stir in the rice to coat well and let the rice and onion cook together for a couple of minutes.

{CONTINUED}

Meanwhile, puree the cilantro, garlic, tomatillos, chile, and salt in a blender with 2 cups broth or water. For 2 cups of rice, you want about 4 cups of liquid; if you need more liquid, add some broth or water.

Pour the green puree into the rice pot and stir well. Bring the mixture to a brisk simmer and let it cook for about 5 minutes.

Put the pot in the oven, uncovered. Bake for 15 minutes. Remove the pot from the oven, cover it with a clean kitchen towel, and let it rest for 15 minutes before serving. (It can sit for up to an hour or be reheated.)

Garnish with a handful of chopped cilantro leaves and a few slivered scallions to heighten the color.

Inside-Out Mangoes

On a hot day in Mexico, the wares from the mango vendor, who sells luscious fresh mangoes impaled on a stick, sliced decoratively and ready to eat, are an outstanding treat. At home, it's traditional to make this inside-out version of cut mangoes.

Mangoes have a big pit in the center. Prepare 6 large mangoes by cutting off 2 fat slices of mango as close to the pit as possible, one on either side. You'll have 2 lush mango halves from each and a pit worth nibbling on. To make the pattern, score the flesh of the mango both lengthwise and crosswise, being careful not to pierce the skin. Then, with your thumbs, push on the skin side to turn the mango half inside out.

Pile the cut mangoes on a platter and serve.

Turkey Deconstructed

Roasted and Braised Turkey with Gravy
Chicken Liver and Apple Stuffing
Spicy Cranberry Chutney

I have a way of cooking turkey that I do year-round. It's unconventional but nonetheless excellent. The problem with roasting a whole turkey is that the breast always dries out before the legs are done. My method solves this problem. First the legs are braised, and a delicious gravy is made from the leg braise. Then the breast is roasted separately, which keeps it moist and juicy. If you feel this is sacrilegious, you can roast a whole turkey for show, but this method is truly worth it.

If this is a Thanksgiving meal, the best strategy is to declare, along with the invitations, that you'll make the turkey, the stuffing, the gravy, and the cranberry chutney and let your guests bring the rest. It's a great day to give up control, provided you're the one who makes sure you'll have the best damn turkey in town.

AMERICANS ABROAD

One year, I was the one making Thanksgiving dinner in
Paris, and for this particular meal, it seemed as if we had every expat in town
descend on our little Paris apartment on the rue St. Jacques. There were going
to be about forty-five of us in all. So I went to my neighborhood butcher,
Charcellet, to get my turkey. They have really good turkeys in France—
small but tasty—and Parisians know about *la fête américaine.* I told the butcher
that I wanted him to take the breasts off, take the legs off, and save me all
the bones. I told him I needed three birds, see you tomorrow, *au revoir.*

I came back the next day and he showed me what he'd done: instead of
cutting off the legs and breasts, he had *deboned* the whole turkeys, as only a
master butcher can do. I marveled. It turned out to be a brilliant solution,
because we have the tiniest oven in the world. At first the birds were flat as
roadkill, but I put salt and pepper all over them, smeared the insides with
garlic and thyme and sage in great quantity, molded them back into a bird
shape, and tied them with string to keep them compact.

Long story short, I found that three compact little re-formed turkeys
would fit side by side in one roasting pan. When they came out of the oven,
I had perfectly cooked roast turkeys with not a speck of unusable anything!
And the cooking time was only an hour and a half.

Our friends said it was the best turkey they'd ever had in their lives.
You could slice through the body as if it were a galantine—all meat and no
stuffing. And this technique applies to every other bird in the world. All
you need is a good butcher or a lot of patience. Simpler by far is the recipe
for the deconstructed bird that follows.

310

Roasted and Braised Turkey with Gravy

I always prefer to cook a smaller turkey. The secret to great flavor is to season the turkey overnight, so begin this process the day before. You can make the broth a day ahead, too.

Have the butcher remove the legs with the thighs attached, cut off the wings, and cut the boneless breast in 2 pieces. While you're at it, ask him to chop up the carcass for your stock. You'll be going home with 2 whole legs with thighs, 2 wings, the skin-on breast in 2 pieces, and a bag of bones. Make sure to get the giblets, too.

FOR THE TURKEY

One 12- to 14-pound turkey,
   cut into six parts (as above)

Salt and pepper

1 bunch sage leaves, chopped

1 small bunch thyme, leaves
   stripped and chopped

6 garlic cloves, smashed to a paste
   with a little salt

2 tablespoons olive oil

FOR THE BROTH

3 pounds turkey carcass and bones
   (or other poultry bones)

1 large onion, peeled, halved, and
   stuck with 1 clove

1 carrot, peeled and chopped

1 celery stalk, chopped

2 bay leaves

2 or 3 slices dried porcini
   mushroom

About 6 quarts water

FOR THE BRAISE

3 tablespoons butter

2 large onions, chopped

Salt and pepper

3 tablespoons all-purpose flour

1 tablespoon tomato paste

1 cup dry red wine

Parsley or watercress sprigs

Put all the turkey pieces out on a big cutting board and season well on both sides with salt and pepper.

{CONTINUED}

Mix the sage, thyme, and garlic in a small bowl, and add the olive oil. Spoon the seasoning mixture over the meat and smear it in well. Put the legs and wings in a container, cover, and refrigerate. Wrap the breasts in plastic and refrigerate.

To make the broth, preheat the oven to 400°F. Put the turkey carcass and bones, onion, carrot, celery, and bay leaves in a roasting pan and into the oven. Roast for about 30 minutes, stirring occasionally, until everything is nicely browned.

Transfer the browned vegetables and bones to a big soup pot. Splash a little water into the roasting pan to dissolve any tasty bits left in the pan, and pour into the pot. Add the dried mushroom and water and bring to a boil. Skim off the scum, turn the heat down to a simmer, and let it cook slowly for 1½ to 2 hours.

Strain the broth through a sieve. You should have about 5 quarts of turkey broth. Cool, then refrigerate; when ready to use, skim off the fat that has risen to the surface.

To make the braise, preheat the oven to 400°F. Put the legs and wings in a large roasting pan, with enough room so they're not crowded. Put the pan in the oven and let the parts roast while you prepare the braising liquid.

In a large skillet over medium heat, melt the butter. Add the onions and season them with salt and pepper. Let them cook gently, stirring occasionally, until softened, about 10 minutes. Turn up the heat and let the onions color a little bit.

With a wooden spoon, stir in the flour and tomato paste and mix well. Add the red wine and 2 cups of the turkey broth and bring to a simmer, stirring as the sauce thickens. Gradually stir in 2 more cups of broth.

Remove the pan of legs and wings from the oven. They should be nicely golden, but not too dark. Pour the braising liquid over the legs. Cover the pan tightly with foil and return to the oven. Reduce the heat to 350°F and let it go for about 1½ hours, or until the legs are tender when tested with a fork. Transfer the legs and wings to a cutting board and let them cool slightly.

Strain the braising liquid through a fine-mesh sieve into a saucepan, skimming off any fat that rises. This will be your gravy. Taste the sauce for seasonings and texture. If it's too thin, reduce it a bit over medium heat until it reaches a consistency you like. Set aside. (The braise can be done hours ahead or the day before and refrigerated.)

When the turkey parts are cool enough to handle, remove the leg meat from the bones in large pieces and tear the meat from the wings. Cut the meat into rough slices and put in a baking dish. Cover and hold at cool room temperature.

Remove the breasts from the refrigerator and let them come to room temperature. The breasts will take only about a half hour to roast, so they can be started up to an hour before dinner in a 375°F oven. Put them in a shallow roasting pan, skin side up, and into the oven. Check at 30 minutes—you want an internal temperature of 140°F. (The temperature will continue to rise as they rest.) Let them rest on a platter, loosely covered, for 15 to 30 minutes before carving.

Shortly before serving, reheat the dark meat in the oven for 10 to 15 minutes, until heated through. Reheat the gravy and put it in a serving bowl.

Slice the turkey breasts on an angle, not too thickly. Arrange the turkey on a warm platter and garnish with parsley or watercress.

Chicken Liver and Apple Stuffing

Since you're cooking the turkey in parts, the stuffing bakes in its own dish. You can bake it hours ahead and reheat it just before dinner.

8 tablespoons (1 stick) butter

2 large onions, finely diced

4 celery stalks, finely diced

Salt and pepper

4 tart apples, peeled, cored, and coarsely chopped

½ pound turkey or chicken livers, chopped

1 tablespoon chopped sage

2 teaspoons chopped thyme

10 cups cubed day-old bread (crusts removed), in ¾-inch pieces

1 cup turkey broth (from preceding recipe)

½ cup heavy cream

2 eggs

Preheat the oven to 350°F. Melt the butter in a large skillet. Add the onions and cook until softened. Add the celery and let it soften, then season with salt and pepper. Add the apples and cook for a minute, then stir in the livers. Add the sage and thyme and turn off the heat.

Put the bread cubes in a large mixing bowl and add the contents of the skillet. Stir together well. Pour in the turkey broth and cream and mix well to moisten the bread. Taste and adjust the seasonings; it should be highly seasoned.

Beat the eggs, and stir them in well. Transfer the stuffing to a buttered shallow baking dish. Bake for about 40 minutes, until golden.

Spicy Cranberry Chutney

This chutney is easy to put together, it keeps for a few days, and you can make it ahead.

3 cups fresh cranberries

¾ cup sugar

One 2-inch piece ginger, peeled and finely slivered

Grated zest of ½ orange

½ teaspoon salt

½ teaspoon cayenne

1 jalapeño, seeded and finely diced

Put the cranberries and sugar in a shallow saucepan or a wide skillet over medium heat, stirring well to dissolve the sugar. Simmer for a few minutes, then add the ginger, orange zest, salt, and cayenne. Continue cooking until the mixture thickens slightly, about 10 minutes.

Stir in the jalapeño. Transfer to a serving bowl and let it cool and jell in the refrigerator before serving.

Auspicious and Delicious

Hair of the Dog, Salty Dog, and Other Grapefruit Drinks
Relish Plate
Quick Bread-and-Butter Pickles
Crab-Stuffed Deviled Eggs
Black-eyed Peas with Ham Hocks and Bacon
Corn Sticks
Lemon Curd Shortbread with Candied Kumquat

This could be an open-house, drop-in kind of spread or a sit-down dinner—a casual meal that goes on throughout the day. It's a convivial way to celebrate in winter, or to welcome in the New Year.

I wasn't raised on dried peas and beans, but once I had my first bowl of pinto beans with bacon, I was hooked. I'm a beanophile to the extent that I was once quoted in an interview as saying: "I really love beans." (I saved the clipping.) Now I'm a full-fledged bean booster. Especially on New Year's Day, when beans seem to be eaten almost worldwide for their good-luck properties. You can make the black-eyed peas the day before and still party on New Year's Eve.

Hair of the Dog, Salty Dog, and Other Grapefruit Drinks

There you are in the middle of winter, in a cold, harsh season, and a little sunshine is only too welcome. Citrus is the true gift of winter and there's something wonderful about freshly squeezed grapefruit juice, mixed with Champagne for a Grapefruit Mimosa, or mixed with vodka for a Salty Dog.

Count on 1 grapefruit per serving; 1 large grapefruit will yield about a cup of juice. There is a world of difference between fresh juice and flash-pasteurized store-bought juice. This is a drink that's all about the freshness, and no, you can't squeeze the fruit the day before. And if your New Year's resolution is a month without alcohol, enjoy a delicious glass of fresh grapefruit juice. You'll feel virtuous and satisfied.

The proportions for a Grapefruit Mimosa are ⅓ grapefruit juice to ⅔ Champagne. Pour the juice into a Champagne glass, then slowly add the Champagne.

To make a Salty Dog, pour 5 ounces grapefruit juice and 1½ ounces vodka, both well chilled, into a glass with a salted rim. Without the salt, the drink is called a Greyhound. To make a Pamplemousse, add the same amount of Pernod to the juice instead of vodka, and don't salt the rim.

Relish Plate

The concept of the old-fashioned relish tray is a nice one, and always a generous gesture. In some restaurants in Italy, you're greeted by vegetable bouquets in water glasses bursting with freshly trimmed raw things like fennel and curly Treviso. American restaurants, especially in New York, always used to bring a relish tray along with the bread basket. It's a habit worth reviving. And nibbling on raw vegetables and an olive or two won't "spoil your dinner," as my mother used to say. It's a welcome thing in all seasons, but especially so during the winter.

Think celery hearts, endive, fennel, carrots, olives, and radishes. Maybe a few spears of half-sour pickle. Even a hothouse-grown cucumber can be refreshing. But in my opinion, raw cauliflower is always a mistake, as are out-of-season cherry tomatoes.

Preparing crudités too far ahead is one of the reasons they have such a bad rap. Though your vegetables will benefit from a brisk cold-water bath, they should be peeled and sliced no more than a few hours before the meal. And, I'm sorry, no sour cream dipping sauce please. The best seasoning for whatever fresh vegetables you choose is a light sprinkling of sea salt.

Quick Bread-and-Butter Pickles

Didn't make pickles last summer? Make these a couple of days (or even a week) ahead; you'll have bright homemade pickles for your table.

6 cucumbers, unpeeled, cut into
   ¼-inch rounds
1 medium onion, sliced very thin
1 sweet red pepper, sliced into
   thin strips
2 tablespoons kosher salt
2 cups cider vinegar

1 cup sugar
½ teaspoon brown mustard seeds
½ teaspoon yellow mustard seeds
½ teaspoon peppercorns
4 allspice berries
2 whole cloves
1 teaspoon turmeric

In a large bowl, combine the cucumbers, onion, and red pepper and toss thoroughly with the salt.

Pour the vinegar into a large saucepan, and stir in the sugar until it is dissolved. Add all the spices, bring the mixture to just under a boil, and simmer for 5 minutes.

Add the cucumber, onion, and pepper mixture. Reduce the heat and simmer, stirring occasionally until the cucumbers begin to change color but are not cooked through, about 5 minutes. Turn off the heat and let stand until the pickles have completely cooled.

Transfer the pickles to a jar, and refrigerate for a few days to let the flavors meld. (Refrigerated, the pickles will keep for weeks.)

Crab-Stuffed Deviled Eggs

I really love deviled eggs—especially these. You can quote me.

1 dozen large organic eggs

1 tablespoon Dijon mustard

¼ cup sour cream or crème fraîche

Generous pinch of cayenne

1 tablespoon snipped chives

½ pound crabmeat, picked over for
shells and cartilage

Juice of ½ lemon

Salt and pepper

Bring a large saucepan of water to a boil. Carefully put the eggs into the water and cook for 10 minutes. Remove the eggs to a bowl of ice water, and when they're cool enough, crack them gently and return to the ice water, so they'll be easier to peel.

Peel the eggs. Cut them in half, scoop out the yolks, and put them in a bowl (reserve the egg white halves). Mash the egg yolks with a fork, and fold in the mustard, sour cream or crème fraîche, cayenne, and half the chives. Gently fold in the crabmeat and lemon juice, and season lightly with salt and pepper. Taste and adjust the seasoning, and spoon the mixture into the waiting egg white halves.

Put the eggs on a platter or two, cover, and refrigerate. Just before serving, sprinkle the eggs with the rest of the chopped chives.

Black-eyed Peas
with Ham Hocks and Bacon

This hearty and traditional dish to welcome in the New Year should be made a day ahead. The flavor will improve.

2 pounds dried black-eyed peas

4 smoked ham hocks, about
   4 pounds

½ pound slab bacon, cut into
   medium dice

2 large onions, halved

1 bay leaf

Large pinch of red pepper flakes

Salt and pepper

8 cups water

Pick over and rinse the peas, and put them in large heavy-bottomed soup pot. Add all the other ingredients and bring to a boil, then skim off the scum and turn down the heat. Simmer very gently for about 2 hours, adding more water if necessary.

When the peas are tender and the ham hock meat is falling from the bone, taste the broth and adjust the seasoning with salt and pepper. Remove the pot from the heat, transfer the black-eyed peas to a shallow container, and refrigerate overnight.

The next day, remove the congealed fat. Reheat the peas, thin with water if necessary, and check the seasoning. Serve them right from the pot.

Corn Sticks

It's nice to make corn bread in an old-fashioned corn stick mold—you get a piece of corn bread that's fluffy and crisp at the same time. If you have a French madeleine pan, you can make little corn cakes. But there's no reason you can't pour the batter into a cast-iron pan and make a traditional corn bread. MAKES ABOUT 24 STICKS

1½ cups organic yellow cornmeal

½ cup all-purpose flour

2 teaspoons baking powder

1 teaspoon baking soda

1 teaspoon salt

2 tablespoons sugar

2 eggs

2 cups buttermilk

6 tablespoons butter,
    melted and cooled

Preheat the oven to 425°F. Put the cornmeal in a large bowl and sift in the flour, baking powder, baking soda, and salt. Add the sugar and stir well.

In a small bowl, beat the eggs, buttermilk, and cooled melted butter. Add to the cornmeal and mix thoroughly.

Generously butter a corn stick pan, and fill each "ear" about three quarters full. Bake for 20 minutes, until nicely browned. Unmold and serve warm. Make additional batches with the rest of the batter.

Lemon Curd Shortbread with Candied Kumquat

You can make these ahead, or even the day before. The lemon curd topping is just a thin layer. MAKES 24 SQUARES

1 cup all-purpose flour

2 tablespoons sugar

A pinch of salt

8 tablespoons (1 stick) unsalted butter

2 large eggs

2 large egg yolks

¾ cup sugar

2 tablespoons cornstarch

Grated zest of 1 lemon

½ cup fresh lemon juice

Candied Kumquat (recipe follows)

Preheat the oven to 350°F. Combine the flour, sugar, and salt in a bowl. Cut in the butter and work the mixture with your hands until it looks like cornmeal. Pat the loose, crumbly mixture onto a large baking pan. The shortbread dough should be about ½ inch thick.

Bake until just lightly browned, about 15 minutes. Meanwhile, to make the curd, whisk together the eggs, yolks, sugar, cornstarch, lemon zest, and juice.

Pour the curd over the crust and bake it for 30 minutes, or until the topping sets. Cool on a rack for at least an hour.

Cut the shortbread into small squares, 1½ to 2 inches. Top each square with a slice of candied kumquat and a little syrup. Arrange on a large serving platter.

Candied Kumquat

Fresh kumquats are lovely sliced raw into salads or lightly candied for desserts.

12 kumquats   ½ cup water
¾ cup sugar

Wash the kumquats. With a sharp knife, slice them crosswise into circles as thin as possible. Pluck out the seeds.

Put the sugar, sliced kumquats, and water in a small saucepan over medium heat. Bring to a simmer, stirring to dissolve the sugar, then reduce the heat to low and cook for about 30 minutes, until a slice you taste seems tender. Remove the pan from the heat and let the kumquats cool in the syrup.

Put the kumquats and syrup in a jar, and they'll keep for a month in the refrigerator.

{VARIATION} KUMQUAT JAM

To make a simple kumquat marmalade, keep cooking the kumquat/sugar mixture until it thickens. You'll have a delicious jam to jar and refrigerate.

Afterword

Give two cooks the same ingredients and the same recipe; it is fascinating to observe how, like handwriting, their results differ. After you cook a dish repeatedly, you begin to understand it. Then you can reinvent it a bit and make it yours. A written recipe can be useful, but sometimes the notes scribbled in the margin are the key to a superlative rendition. Each new version may inspire improvisation based on fresh understanding. It doesn't have to be as dramatic as all that, but such exciting minor epiphanies keep cooking lively.

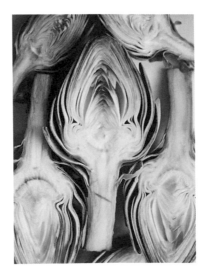

Acknowledgments

Thanks to the wonderful folks at Artisan, especially Peter Workman, Ann Bramson, Trent Duffy, Amy Corley, Judith Sutton, Barbara Peragine, Jan Derevjanik, Nancy Murray, and Erin Sainz.

Thanks to all the extraordinary people at Canal House: Christopher Hirsheimer and Melissa Hamilton, Jim Hirsheimer, Jim Hamilton, Michael Hagerty, Julie Sprosser, Rachel Weinreb, and Elizabeth May. Thanks to John Carloftis.

Merci mille fois to Dorothy Kalins and Dorothy Kalins Ink. Thanks to Roger Sherman, Lincoln Sherman, Sandrine Lago, and Gigi.

Thanks to Katherine Cowles, angel and agent.

Thanks to Barbara Tanis Design.

Thanks to everyone at Chez Panisse, especially Alice. Also to Jean-Pierre Moullé, Jérôme Waag, Beth Wells, Cal Peternell, Nathan Alderson, Amy Dencler, Ryan Childs, Aaron Rocchino, Nico Monday, and Gordon Heyder.

Thanks to Barbara Tanis, Stuart Busch, Fabrizia Lanza, Ignacio Mattos and Gaby Plater, Richard Gilbert and Gilbert Pilgram, Bruce Nauman, Susan Rothenberg, and Maggie Trakas for friendship and feasting.

Thanks to Bob Cannard, salt of the earth.

Thanks to the Chino family for farming the land.

Thanks to Eleanor and Ray Must, for teaching me about figs and quinces, early on.

Thanks to Steven Barclay and Garth Bixler, Joan Simon and Alan Kennedy, Seen Lippert and Fred Landman, Kevin West, Angelo Garro, Kenny Parker, Michael and Sylvie Sullivan, Richard and Deidre Gordon, Camille Labro, David Lebovitz and Romain Pellas, Michael and Jill Wild, David Lindsey, Claire Ptak, Susie and David Ritch, Tony Oltranti and Bob Carrau, generous spirits and table mates.

Thanks to Peggy Knickerbocker, Niloufer Ichaporia King, Caroline Gordon, Sue Murphy, Kate Coleman, Carol Lewitt, Davia Nelson, Sharon Jones, Alta Tingle, Clare Bell, and Margo Channing. *Vive les femmes!*

And finally, but far from least, abiding thanks to Randal Breski.

Index